LEADERSHIP

Sanjay Saxena
Reader
Department of Management
School of Management Sciences
Varanasi

Purnima Awasthi
Assistant Professor
Department of Psychology
Faculty of Social Sciences
Banaras Hindu University
Varanasi

PHI Learning Private Limited
Delhi-110092
2026

In fond memory of ***Shri Asoke K. Ghosh*** *(October 1942 – February 2024), Founder Chairman and Managing Director of PHI Learning, whose vision endlessly inspires.*

The Legacy Continues....

Published by Pushpita Ghosh, PHI Learning Private Limited, Rimjhim House, 111, Patparganj Industrial Estate, Delhi-110092 and Printed by Syndicate Binders, A-20, Hosiery Complex, Noida, Phase-II Extension, Noida-201305 (N.C.R. Delhi).

₹750.00

LEADERSHIP
Sanjay Saxena and Purnima Awasthi

ISBN-978-81-203-3929-3 (Print Book)
ISBN-978-93-5443-690-1 (e-Book)

The export rights of the book are vested solely with the publisher.

Contents

Preface .... *ix*
Acknowledgements .... *xi*

SECTION I: CONCEPTUAL FRAMEWORK

Chapter 1 **Leadership: An Overview** **3–5**

Chapter 2 **Leadership Thoughts and Definitions** **6–9**

Chapter 3 **Leader vs Non-leader** **10–12**

Chapter 4 **Leadership vs Management** **13–17**
Take Risk vs Eliminate Risk *15*
Focus on People vs Focus on System *15*
Aligning and Inspiring vs Organizing and Controlling *15*
Providing Direction *16*
Creation of Organizational DNA *16*

Chapter 5 **Leadership Styles** **18–19**
Positive or Negative Motivation *18*
Decision-making Style *19*
Task Operation and Employee Orientation *19*

Chapter 6 **Situational Leadership** **20–26**
Situational Leaders *21*
Characteristics of Situational Leaders *21*
Followers *22*
Followership Patterns *23*

What Followers Expect from a Leader? *24*
Honesty *25*
Competence *25*
Forward Looking *25*
Inspiring *25*
Leadership Situation *25*
Leader-members Relations *25*
Task Structure *25*
Position Power *26*
What Should be an Appropriate Style of Leadership? *26*

Chapter 7 Transactional and Transformational Leadership 27–30
Transactional Leaders *27*
Transformational Leaders *27*
Transformational Leaders Possess Charisma *28*
Key Characteristics of Charismatic Leader *28*
What Do Charismatic Leaders Do? *29*
Four Powers of Transformational Leaders *29*

Chapter 8 Leadership Behaviour at Workplace 31–35
Task Oriented Leadership Behaviour *32*
Relationship Oriented Leadership Behaviour *34*

Chapter 9 Leadership in Indian Culture 36–38
What Should be the Appropriate Leadership Style in Indian Culture? *38*

Chapter 10 World-class Organization 39–45
Attributes of World-class Organizations 39
World-class Organizations' Needs *41*
High Performing World-Class Organizations *42*
Employee Involvement *43*
Self Directing Teams *43*
Integrated Production Technology *43*
Learning Organizations *43*
Total Quality Management *44*
High-performance Gracious Culture *44*
Creative Human Resource Management *44*
Society Based Focus *44*
Open Climate *45*

Chapter 11 Strategic Leadership Cycle 46–47

SECTION II: LEADER AS INTEGRATED HUMAN BEING

Chapter 12 Power of Leaders 51–54

Chapter 13 Personal Paradigm 55–57

Chapter 14 Physical Acumen 58–63
Appearance and Artifacts *58*
Communication *59*
Spoken Communication Tool Kit *60*
Eye Contact *60*
Body Language *60*
Style and Register *60*
Paralanguage/Vocalic *60*
Tips for Effective Use of Non-verbal Communication *62*
Tips to Develop Physical Acumen *62*

Chapter 15 Mental Acumen 64–69
Sleep well *66*

Chapter 16 Emotional Acumen 70–103
Emotional Autonomy *71*
Mission *71*
How to Find Contents for Personal Mission *72*
Guidelines to Write Personal Mission Statement 73
Example of Personal Mission Statement *74*
Roles and Goals *74*
Guidelines to Set Personal Goals *75*
Attitude *75*
Various Ways to Assure Positive Attitude *75*
Discipline *77*
Invincible Thinking *78*
Values *78*
Values, Accomplishment, and Our Psychological Energies *80*
Core Values of a Leader *80*
Self-esteem *81*
Consequences of Low Self-esteem *82*
Proactivity *85*
Proactive Language *86*
Internal and External Focus *87*
Assertive Behaviour *87*
Passive Behaviour *87*
Aggressive Behaviour *88*
Assertive Behaviour *88*
Spirituality *88*
Generating Excellence in Work *89*
Contribution *91*
Integration *92*
Three Modes of Material Nature *92*
Emotional Reciprocation *94*
Mutual Trust *95*
How to Become Trustworthy? *96*
Affection *98*

Commitment *98*
Sincerity *99*
Cooperation *99*
Courtesy *100*
Modesty *101*
Synergistic Agreement *101*
Egocentric Mindset *102*
Flaccid Mindset *102*
Stubborn Mindset *102*
Synergistic Mindset *102*

Chapter 17 Tips to Improve Interpersonal Skills 104–105

Chapter 18 Vitality of Relationships 106–107

Chapter 19 Development of Good Habits 108–112
Habits *108*
Acquiring Leadership Competences as Habits *108*
How to Develop Good Habits? *110*
Tips to Reprogram our Unconscious Mind *110*
Leaders' Language *111*

SECTION III: COURSE OF ACTION

Chapter 20 Leadership Functions 115–116

Chapter 21 Envisioning and Alignment 117–120
Vision *118*
Important Characteristics of Effective Vision *118*
Power of Vision *119*
Communicating Vision *119*
Strategic Direction *120*

Chapter 22 Emotional Transition 121–123
Denial *122*
Overcoming Denial *122*
Resistance *122*
Overcoming Resistance *122*
Exploration *123*
Response to Exploration *123*
Commitment *123*
Response to Commitment *123*

Chapter 23 Organizational Mission 124–126
Characteristics of the Effective Mission *125*
Spiritual Mission *125*

Chapter 24 Mentorship 127–130
What is Mentoring? *127*
Attributes of a Successful Mentor *128*
Role of a Mentor *128*

Identify Hidden Potential and Development Needs *130*
Coaching Methodology *130*
Spiritual Dimensions in Mentoring *130*

Chapter 25 Fostering Teamwork 131–142
What is a Team? *131*
Team Fundamentals *133*
Small Number *133*
Complementary Skills *134*
Individual Accountability and Personal Growth *135*
Commitment to Team's Mission and Goals *135*
Commitment to a Common Approach *136*
Mutual Accountability *136*
Performance Results *136*
Leaders' Behaviour and Attitude Fostering Teamwork *137*
High Performance Teams *142*

Chapter 26 Motivation 143–152
What is motivation? *143*
What Motivate Employees? *143*
Csikszentimihalyi's Concept of "Flow" Experiences *144*
The Concept of Self-systems *144*
Bandura's Social Cognitive Theory *144*
How to Enhance Motivation? *145*
Allow Employees Full Autonomy and Control *145*
Create Learning Opportunities *146*
Encourage Teamwork *146*
Ensure Positive Work Environment *146*
Management by Objective *147*
Participative Management *147*
Job Enrichment and Redesign *147*
Modified Work Schedule *147*
Offer Training Opportunities *147*
Provide On-the-job Coaching *148*
Provide a Challenging Work *148*
Cultivate an Atmosphere of Respect *148*
Demotivators *148*
A Refreshing Approach to Motivation *150*
Spiritual Dimensions in Motivation *151*

Chapter 27 Empowerment 153–157
Advantages of Empowerment *155*
Why Employee Empowerment Fails? *156*

Chapter 28 Leading Change 158–166
Why Change? *158*
Driving Forces of Organizational Change *160*
What to Change? *161*

Resistance to Change *162*
Role of a Leader in Overcoming Resistance to Change *162*
The Change Process *163*

Chapter 29 Shaping Organizational Culture 167–179
Significance of Organizational Culture *168*
Internal Integration *169*
External Adaptation *169*
Culture for Excellence *169*
Characteristics of Low Performance Culture *170*
Organizational Environments *172*
Commitment *172*
Relationships *173*
Shared Values and Beliefs *173*
High Performance Culture on the Basis of Admirable Environment and Positive Performance *174*
Dictatorial Culture *174*
Frightening Culture *174*
Fruitless Culture *175*
High Performance Organizational Culture *175*
Organizational Transcendence *176*
Gracious Work Culture *177*
Why Change in Organizational Culture is Difficult? *177*
How to Bring Changes in Organizational Culture? *177*
Criteria for Successful Cultural Change *178*
Key factor in Culture Change *178*

APPENDICES

1. *Leadership Qualities* *183*
2. *Emotional Autonomy* *185*
3. *Emotional Reciprocation* *187*
4. *Change Agent* *189*
5. *Assessment of Leadership Practices in the Organization* *191*
6. *Assessment of Team Effectiveness* *194*

References *197–200*

Index *201–204*

Preface

The world is crying for leaders. Business organizations require leaders at every level to sustain their growth and win the competition. The big questions are: Who are these leaders? What are their roles in the business organizations? How can they create the difference and why do we require them? What difference can they make to this world? What should be their characteristics?

Business organizations want leaders, who are value-driven personalities, who can control the circumstances by making things happen, develop organization's, DNA (mission, vision and ethical values), win the employees' commitment with the DNA, develop better paradigm with proper work culture and lead people towards the achievement of organizational vision, mission and objectives.

The purpose of the text is implied by its title "Leadership". It is designed for the existing and future business executives at front, middle and top levels to add leadership qualities and approaches in their managerial personality.

The reader who masters this text will acquire an overview of the research literature about leadership. In addition, the reader will acquire a feel for how leadership is practised in organizational settings and also gain insights and information to develop leadership traits and skills.

It is important to note that this book is not intended to duplicate or substitute for an organizational behaviour text. Our approach, however, is to emphasize skills development, diagnosis and prescription rather than duplicating basic descriptions of concepts and theories.

This book is intended to provide the knowledge of best leadership properties and practices to the entrepreneurs, business managers, administrators, teachers, and students (future managers) so that they can be transformed into world-class leaders that in turn will establish Indian organizations on global platform.

To become a world-class leader, a person has to understand deeply the characteristics of a leader, role of leaders, the differences between leadership and managerial approaches, and what the leadership functions are in the organizations. This book provides the same.

The present book follows the leadership development model designed by the authors. This model contains three sections, namely conceptual framework, leader as an integrated human being, and courses of action in organizations, respectively.

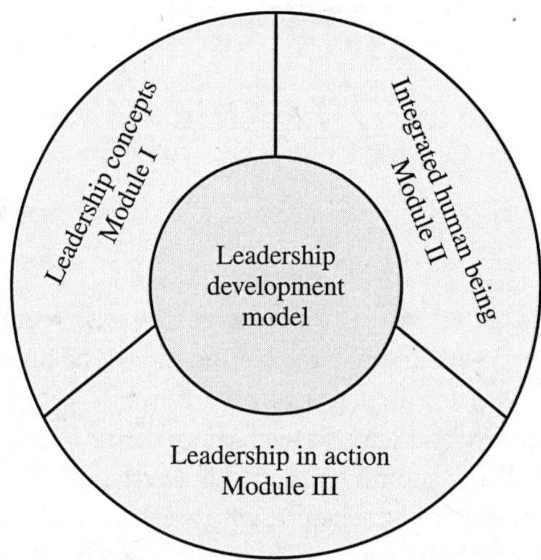

Leadership Development Model

The first section provides modern concepts and different perspectives of leadership. The readers will become acquainted with the minuscule differences between leaders and non-leaders, approaches of managers and leaders, the concepts of transactional, situational and transformational leadership, leadership behaviour at workplace and the effect of culture on it.

The second section is all about the development of person as an integrated human being. A world-class leader must be of a value-driven personality and possess certain traits, potentials, skills, knowledge and internal locus of control to generate his/her strength, wisdom, direction and power to take and actions. This section also emphasizes the development of interpersonal skills to build productive relationship with people.

The third section describes different courses of action that a leader has to take in the real-life situation. All the functions of leadership are dealt with in detail.

Sanjay Saxena
Purnima Awasthi

Acknowledgements

We would like to extend our deep sense of gratitude to our esteemed teachers and eminent scholars Professor R.C. Mishra, Professor A.K. Srivastava, and Professor I.L. Singh (Head), Department of Psychology, Banaras Hindu University, for their continuous support and encouragement for the production of this work. They are role models for us and always a motivating force behind all our endeavours.

Vocabulary falls short of words to convey our indebtedness to Proffessor N. Prasad and Professor A.K. Ghosh, Department of Metallurgical Engineering, Institute of Technology, Banaras Hindu University, Varanasi. They have offered their valuable suggestions and helpful discussion during the prepration of this manuscript.

We are obliged to Dr. M.P. Singh, Executive Secretary, School of Management Sciences, Varanasi, and Professor P.N. Jha, Director, School of Management Sciences, Varanasi, for their constant inspiration, emotional and infrastructural support to complete this book.

We are extremely thankful to Mr. Uttam Kumar Das for preparing all the diagrams incorporated in this book.

We are unable to express our deep feelings for our respected parents, in-laws, brothers and sisters and lovely daughters Lipi and Saumya, for their inestimable love, affection and emotional support.

Sanjay Saxena
Purnima Awasthi

SECTION I

CONCEPTUAL FRAMEWORK

1

Leadership: An Overview

The four historical perspectives of leadership include, trait, behaviour, contingency and transformation. The trait perspective suggests that leaders are born, not made. The basic assumption is that a great human can be a great leader, but very few seem to be convinced that inherent personality traits are the sole determinants of leadership capability and success. Sir Stogdill's review of hundreds of trait studies in 1948, revealed that there are five important distinguishing factors associated with successful leaders. These factors are: capacity, achievement, responsibility, participation, and status.

A behavioural perspective on leadership focuses on what a leader does. Two classic leadership studies conducted by Universities of Ohio State, and Michigan, in the 1950s and 1960s, respectively, made distinction between task-oriented and person-oriented leadership behaviour. The task-oriented behaviour of a leader is important to increase efficiency and to achieve group goals. The task orientation concentration is given on defining roles, providing structures, directing activities, communicating information, scheduling, etc. On the other hand, the person-orientation is equally important and it relates to consideration of people's feelings, building of mutual trust, respect for people's ideas, and attitudes.

Various researches on the leaders' behaviour in different situations have found that specific leadership behaviour is effective in some circumstances and may be ineffective under different conditions. Thus, the effectiveness of leadership behaviour is contingent upon organizational situations. The contingency perspective explains the relationship between leadership styles and effectiveness in specific situations. The contingency approach suggests that there is no one best way of leadership. It means "it depends." The contingency approaches seek to delineate the characteristics of situations, followers and examine the leadership styles that can be used effectively.

One of the primary responsibilities of the transformational leader is to develop peoples' abilities and enable them to reach their full potential. They identify the hidden potential of their employees and shape them through nurturing leadership. They perform their roles as teacher, coach, and mentor to develop their subordinates. Transformational leadership involves in inspiring the employees. The leaders understand that getting people to accomplish something is much easier if they have the motivation to do so. Therefore, leaders "breathe life into the people through proper nurturing rather than just managing them."

Extensive researches have shown that leadership is an observable and learnable set of practices. It is not something mystical that cannot be understood by ordinary people. Given the opportunity, feedback, and practice, those with the desire and persistence to lead can improve their ability to do so. A good leader develops through a never ending process of self-study, education, training, experience, inventive thinking and contemplation.

To inspire the workers into higher levels of teamwork, there are certain things that must be, known, and, done (that are characteristics, concepts, and actions). These do not come naturally, but are acquired through continual work and study. Good leaders are continually working and studying to improve their leadership skills; they are not resting on their laurels.

Without effective leadership at every level in private and public organizations, it is difficult to sustain profitability, productivity, quality, and good customer services. Researchers have demonstrated that leadership does make a difference in dozens of different ways. In various organizations top management and other stakeholders believe that without effective leadership the organization cannot remain competitive.

Nowadays, most organizations are underled and overmanaged. Leadership must be developed in organizations because the people in charge are too concerned with keeping things on-time and on-budget and with doing what was done yesterday, only doing it better (Kotter 1990). As indicated in Table 1.1 the problem for today's organizations is that there are too many people doing just management, few providing leadership, and fewer who have integrated the skills and qualities needed for meeting both leadership and management challenges.

TABLE 1.1 Leader Manager Grid

Managerial Skills		Leadership Skills	
		Weak	*Strong*
	Strong	Many	Almost none
	Weak	Too many	Very few

In this highly competitive era of globalization where business organizations are striving to develop competence in order to move ahead of competitors, effective leadership at all levels can contribute successfully for the purpose. A leader has to detach himself or herself from day to day bottom line working and to move above the organizational paradigm to have the helicopteric view of the organization as a whole between the horizons. He or she should focus on the direction towards which organization is moving and make corrections if required. His or her prime job is to review the strategic position of the organization in the environment and put it into right path to reach at desired destination. An appropriate organizational culture is required to deploy available resources optimally, and to develop competences and core competences. Leadership at all levels is obligatory to develop proper organizational culture. An organization having people with leadership skills can achieve higher degree of robustness and pose strong challenges in front of competitors to imitate its competencies.

Any organization which is satisfied with mediocre performance will be able to survive with managers only. However, for organizations who want to distinguish themselves from others and to be excellent, leadership is mandatory. Truly excellent companies obtained their way through passionate leadership.

There is tremendous demand for world-class leader-managers who know when to lead and when to manage? Leaders lead people and develop proper work culture to generate excellence in all the organizational performances; whereas managers manage things, plan activities, involved in organizing and controlling to stabilize the environment and increase the productivity.

2

Leadership Thoughts and Definitions

Leadership has been identified as a multidimensional non-linear process, a new and complex science. The truth about leadership is that it is a quality and one that is earned, rather than a qualification.

True leaders have the ability to craft other people to perform what they do not want to, and like it.

Many leaders, who concern themselves with planning, controlling, directing and communicating; and excel in these, are in fact just good managers and possibly not good leaders at all. Leadership is probably best described as the honour granted to an individual by those who subscribe to his/her leadership.

Many people wrongly perceive a leader as the senior most or most powerful person in an organization or socio-political setting. It is quite different from this widely held belief. Leadership is a highly multidimensional phenomenon, which can be understood and analyzed from different perspectives. In order to have a comprehensive understanding of this phenomenon, let us examine it from different standpoints:

Managerial perspective

Leadership complements management; it does not replace it. Once companies understand the fundamental difference between leadership and management, they groom their top people to provide both (Kotter 1990).

From managerial point of view leadership is an important element of the directing function of management. The leaders induce confidence and passion through nurturing leadership in their subordinates to perform the work excellently. They have a sense of responsibility to direct the actions of others in carrying out the organizational purposes by being accountable for success or failure.

Process perspective

Leadership is an influence process. It is a process in which one person sets the purpose or direction for one or more persons, and gets them to move along together with him and with each other in that direction with competence and full commitment.

An authentic leader is not only a visionary, but also functions in the way, a helicopter does. He or she flies high to get the big picture, but can quickly zoom down into a specific trouble spot and attend to minuscule details.

Leadership is always oriented towards some goal. If the goal is improper the effectiveness will not be there, no matter how efficiently the organization is managed. Great leadership entails a deep sense of ethical values and societal goals.

Leadership is also about developing high performing culture that involves development of organizational DNA (vision, mission and values), aligning people with the same, generate their commitment, and influence and inspire the group of people for higher performances. Great leaders do not stay in their offices; instead they always go to their people and move along with them. Leaders bring others to a place they have not been before (Warren and Nanus 1985).

Leadership is not about making friends and influencing people, that is sales manship. It is the lifting of man's vision to higher sights, and the raising of man's personality beyond its normal limitations (Drucker 1992). This can only be done through nurturing leadership.

Property perspective

Set of characteristics attributed to individuals who are perceived to be leaders. There is no finishing line in leadership development, best leaders are always preparing for tomorrow.

True leaders are always enthusiastic and with full of passion and they never ever pretend to look cold. People who pretend to look cold possess some dictator's property in them. Also true leaders do not want to be nice persons; instead they are like a mirror that always reflects real picture. They believe that leadership is about being right and being strong. Once Ex British Prime Minister Tony Blair (2000) said in his speech that "the art of leadership is saying no, not yes. It is very easy to say yes." But above all, leaders must feel themselves accountable for what is happening around. Persons with sense of accountability are actually the world-class individuals in real sense. We cannot command or influence other's behaviour unless we are able to control ourself. Good leaders always compete with themselves and follow laser beam strategy to be focused on targets. Their journey of excellence never stops.

Transformational perspective

The transformational leader is one who commits people to action, who converts followers into leaders and who may convert leaders into agents of change. Leaders empower others to translate intention into reality and sustain it. The action is pulling rather than pushing. He/she motivates by identification, rather than through rewards and punishment. Leading is a responsibility, and the effectiveness of this responsibility is reflected in the attitudes of the followers. Leadership is very much distinct from supervision, which involves keeping a grasp on the situation and ensuring that plans and policies are implemented properly by giving instructions and inspecting the accomplishment of a task.

Relationship perspective

One result of this transformation in the concept of leadership has been the rethinking of leadership definitions. Rost (1993) of University of San Diego is one of the most popular writers in recognizing the shift from the industrial concept of leadership (leader-centred view) to a paradigm he calls the post-industrial concept of leadership. In his book *Leadership for the Twenty-First Century*, he articulates a definition of leadership based on this post-industrial perspective. A definition he believes is more consistent with contemporary organizational life. Rost's definition says that leadership is an influence relationship among leaders and followers who intend real changes that reflect their mutual purposes.

This contemporary definition is composed of four basic components, each of which is essential and must be present if a particular relationship is to be called leadership:

1. The relationship is based on influence. This influence is multi-directional, meaning that influence can go any way (not necessarily top to down), and the influence attempts must not be coercive. Therefore, the relationship is not based on authority, but rather persuasion.
2. Leaders and followers are the people in this relationship. If leadership is defined as a relationship, then both leaders and followers are doing leadership. We do not say that all players in this relationship are equal, but do say that all active players practice influence. Typically there is more than one follower and more than one leader in this arrangement.
3. Leaders and followers intend real changes. Intend means that the leaders and followers promote and purposefully seek changes. Real means that the changes intended by the leaders and followers must be substantial.
4. The changes the leaders and followers intend reflect their mutual purposes. The key is that the desired changes must not only reflect the wishes of the leader but also the desires of the followers (Rost 1993).

Rost reminds us that leadership is not what leaders do; rather, leadership is what leaders and followers do together for the collective good. In today's society, leaders operate in a shared-power environment with followers. No longer does a single leader have all the answers and the power to make substantial changes. Instead, today we live in a world where many people participate in leadership, some as leaders and others as followers. Only when we all work together we can bring successful changes for our mutual purposes.

Many organizational theorists would agree that Rost's definition is more consistent with the type of leadership needed in contemporary society. Slowly scholars and practitioners alike are giving up the old ways of leadership, the industrial paradigm. This traditional approach to leadership is characterized by a top to down philosophy, where the leader is decisive, efficient, unemotional and in-control. The changes in the way, we view leadership can also be found in other disciplines where descriptions of our world are objective, single, mechanical, hierarchical and controllable. The post-industrial paradigm, on the other hand, is characterized by networks of mind, power-sharing facilitation, and empowerment. The best leaders do not want to be applauded by people. There physical presence merely exists but their aroma is always present in the environment. They take the blame on their shoulders and share the success because they know the power of "we". Therefore, the essence of leadership is not the leader, but the relationship.

Thus, we can conclude that the leader is a person who sets attractive goals and has the ability to attract followers, or constituents, who share those goals. Leadership is the capability and process to influence a group non-coercively towards achievement of goals. It is a process, which bridges the gap between the expectations and the current reality. Leadership is the practice of influence that stimulates subordinates or followers to do their best towards the achievement of the desired goals. Leadership is all about developing relationship with followers, transforming them into leaders or agents of change, empowering them, and mutually bringing substantial changes for the organizational development.

Finally, we consider a leader as a person who has right blend of physical, mental and emotional acumen and he/she is the one who creates vision; align people with the same; develop relationship with followers to collectively achieve mutual purposes; involved in mentoring his followers; empower and motivate followers to take initiatives and decisions; mutually bring substantial changes in the organization and strive to develop world-class organizational culture.

3

Leader vs Non-leader

The differences between a leader's and non-leader's approaches can be better understood by examining their personal traits, behaviour at workplace, and relationship building attitude. It is worth mentioning here that no person is leader or non-leader in absolute terms instead there exits a mix of both the leader and non-leader attributes in various percentages. One should first assess himself on various leadership dimensions, then contemplate the knowledge of leadership and assimilate it in their personality to enhance leadership qualities. Tables 3.1, 3.2, and 3.3 present the differences between leader and non-leader on the basis of personal traits, behaviour at work place, and relationship building attitude, respectively.

TABLE 3.1 Difference between a Leader and a Non-leader on the Basis of Personal Traits

Leaders	*Non-leaders*
Proactive: They have a sense of responsibility. They take the blame on their shoulder. Shapes the ideas rather then responding to them. They have a passion to develop vision and mission of the organization. They consider themselves accountable for what is happening in the organization. Focused on organizational goals.	**Passive:** Always tries to be out of picture and escape from being accountable. Find someone to blame. Goals arise from necessities rather than desires. Focused on self.

(Contd.)

TABLE 3.1 Difference between a Leader and a Non-leader on the Basis of Personal Traits (*Contd.*)

Leaders	*Non-leaders*
Empathic listener: Listen people to understand them fully and deeply. Like to get influenced by others and view listening as learning opportunity.	**Filtered listening:** Listen people to assess that they agree or disagree with them. Listen people just to give them reply. Scared of getting influenced by others and view listening as losing control.
Emotionally independent: Take emotional strength from their personal paradigm. Guided by their values.	**Emotionally dependent:** Take their emotional strength from friends, family, spouse and their possessions, etc. Guided by others' weaknesses.
Resilient: Do not crumble with setbacks. Copes with adverse situation quickly.	**Feeble:** Get shattered with failures.
Adaptable: Adapt the changes.	**Stiff:** Rigid in adapting changes.
Self-confident: Highly self-assured in their judgement, decisions and capabilities.	**Indecisive:** Unable to make decision. Poor belief in their capability.
Honest: Truthful, credible and non-deceptive. Honesty is foundation of trust between leaders and followers.	**Erratic:** Inconsistent behaviour. Sometime use power and authority deceptively.
Compassionate: Have sympathy for people who are suffering and desire to help them.	**Icy:** Covered with thick sheet of selfish attitude.
Ask tough questions to themselves: Can we run a business on ethical values?	Afraid to face tough questions.
Believe in creating history.	Follow the history.

TABLE 3.2 Deffirence between a Leader and a Non-leader on the Basis of Behaviour at Workplace

Leaders	*Non-leaders*
Change agent: Bring changes in the system for betterment and control their circumstances. Engage in developing fresh approaches.	**Preserver:** Maintains current system and get along with that. Controlled by their circumstances.
Mentor: A coach with open doors; problem solver and advise-giver; cheer leader. Available for help. Prefer personal and eyeball-to-eyeball contact.	**Dictator:** Gives order to staff. Hard to reach from below. Prefer memos, long reports and committees.

TABLE 3.3 Difference between a Leader and a Non-leader on Relationship Building Attitude

Leaders	*Non-leaders*
Straightforward: Knows why and when to say no and say's no whenever required. Want to be a right person.	**Manipulative:** Always say yes to create good image of him. Lack of consistency between saying and thinking. Want to be a nice person in the eyes of others.
Trusts people	Trusts only words and numbers on paper
Good listener: Give others chance to express their problems, feelings, expectations, and ideas.	**Good talker:** Always involved in expressing his/her own problems, ideas, ambitions and expectations.
Openness: Share information with subordinates. Clean hearted.	**Secrecy:** Try to hide information from subordinates.
Predictable: Consistent and credible to his/her subordinates.	**Unpredictable:** says what they think other want to hear.
Attached: Rich in emotional content when dealing with others.	**Detached:** Emotions for self.
Thinks about mutual benefits while dealing with others.	Thinks about own benefits.
Handle conflict with passion.	Avoid conflict (I am not in picture).
Empower subordinates.	Scared of loosing power.
Worried about his/her role.	Worried about his/her position.

4

Leadership vs Management

To understand leadership, it is important to grab the difference between leadership and management. Broadly speaking leadership deals with the interpersonal behaviour dynamics and change aspects of the manager's job, whereas planning, organizing, and controlling concentrates administrative aspects. According to current thinking leadership deals with change, inspiration, motivation, and influence. In contrast, management deals more with maintaining equilibrium and the status quo. Managers concentrate on bottom line to stabilize systems within the paradigm, whereas leaders look into the horizons to bring required changes in the organization. The main difference between a manager and a leader is in the vision and power. Leaders always carry vision and generate their power from people, whereas managers may not have vision and generate their power from their position.

We can manage materials but cannot really manage human beings as they have their own thoughts and emotions, they can be guided or led only. Therefore, leaders concentrate on guiding or leading people towards the right destination.

Management essentially copes with complexity; leadership copes with change (Kotter 1990). Leadership makes sure that the ladders we are climbing are leaning against the right wall, management makes sure we are climbing the ladders in the most efficient ways possible (Covey 1989).

According to Kotter (1990), leaders are not the replacement of managers but leadership and management are two distinctive and complementary systems of action, each has its own function and characteristic activities, both necessary for success in an increasing complex and volatile business environment.

Leadership begins where management ends, where systems of reward, punishment and control give way to innovation, empowerment, individual character, and the courage of conviction. Once the companies understand the fundamental difference between leadership and management, they groom their top people to provide both.

Managers are the people who have been given the assignment to lead others, but lack the skills or motivation to do so, whereas leadership is the honour granted to a person by his/her subordinates.

Global leader-managers are the people who are equally competent in both the managerial and leadership capabilities. Table 4.1 presents the distinction between complementary managerial and leadership systems of action.

TABLE 4.1 Distinction between Complementary Managerial and Leadership Systems of Action

Leaders	*Managers*
Challenges the existing systems	Accepts status quo
Takes risks by making changes	Eliminates risks by preserving the system
Innovates	Administers, creates order
Develops	Maintains
Ask what and why	Asks How and When
Does right things	Does things right
Focus on people	Focus on system
Inspire trust	Relies on control
Empower	Control
Initiates and originates potential	Responds and reacts to performance
Copes with change	Copes with complexity
Aligns people to take the initiative	Organize people around already taken initiatives
Inspires and motivates	Controls and solves problems
Direction–creating vision and strategy by keeping an eye on horizon	Planning and budgeting by keeping an eye on bottom line
Connects emotionally (heart)	Keep emotional distance (expert mind)
Tag line "Let me show you how you can use these rules to your advantage"	Tag line "I implement the rules"
Provides the tools and training, then allows employees to "do it" by letting go	Closely supervise the doing
Facilitates employees in resolving problems	Solves problems
Influences the way people think, at the core is trust	People "do" because they are told to "do"

Take Risk vs Eliminate Risk

Global leader-managers in their leader's role are the agents of change and they see organization not as what it is but as what it can be. They challenge the existing system and take initiatives with innovative ideas to develop the organization. They take risk of disrupting the systems. They ask what improvements are required to achieve the mission of the organization and why those are required? With appropriate vision and mission they have correct sense of purpose and direction of the organization and they do right things to achieve the same.

After disrupting the existing system of the organization, leader-managers quickly come back to their managerial role to eliminate risks, administer and maintain the system to increase productivity. By asking how and when to do the different activities, and through planning, organizing, and controlling functions they try to do things right.

Focus on People vs Focus on System

The leaders focus their efforts on the development of the people of the organization. They align people with vision and mission of the organization, inspire them to take the initiatives to implement desired changes in the organization and also motivate them to achieve the organizational goals. They empower their employees to take decisions and develop trust among them. Through mentoring, coaching and teaching they identify and develop the potential of their people. Task is to transform the followers into leaders and finally into agents of change.

Managers keep their focus on the system in order to develop and maintain efficient productive systems in the organization. They organize activities; assign job responsibilities to the people, develop effective control mechanisms, manage resources as well as budget and plan.

Aligning and Inspiring vs Organizing and Controlling

There are clear advantages of aligning and inspiring people over organizing them towards predetermined goals and putting managerial controls on their activities. Through alignment, leaders pull people with them, develop informal and trustful relationship, expand energy and win their commitment, that in turn generate huge amount of psychological energy in the environment to produce excellent performances. On the other hand, in organizing people manager asks for people's compliance rather then commitment and with more controls, managers push people that constrains their energy and results in lack of initiatives from subordinates. All the efforts of aligning people with already taken initiatives and organize people around them are considered as selling the initiatives. Leaders prepare people to take initiatives by themselves for the required changes in the organization. Therefore, they start aligning people before taking any initiative for change and encourage them to take the initiatives to bring change. In the world-class organizations leaders go beyond the boundaries of their organizations and align all the stakeholders to generate wealth for everyone in the society.

Management involves organizing a structure to accomplish the plan; staffing the structure with employees; and developing policies, procedures, and systems to direct employees and monitor implementation of the plan. Managers are thinkers and subordinates are doers. Leadership is concerned instead with communicating the vision and developing a shared culture and set of core values that can lead to desired future state. This involves followers and leaders both as thinkers and doers. Whereas the vision describes the destination, the culture and values help define the journey towards it.

Managers organize by separating people into specialities and functions, with boundaries separating them by departmental and hierarchical levels. Leaders break down boundaries so people know what others are doing, can coordinate easily, and feel a sense of teamwork, equity for achieving desired objectives. Rather than directing and controlling the employees, leadership is concerned with helping others to grow so that they can fully contribute in achieving the vision.

Providing Direction

Both leadership and management are concerned with providing direction for the organization, but there are differences. Management focuses on establishing detailed plans and schedules for achieving specific results, and allocating resources to accomplish the plans.

Leadership calls for creating the vision of the future and developing farsighted strategies for producing the changes needed to achieve that vision. Whereas management calls for keeping an eye on the bottom line and short-term results, leadership means keeping an eye on the horizon and long-term future.

Creation of Organizational DNA

Organizational DNA is the main source behind all kind of success in the organization in terms of making the organization robust, converting organizational resources into competences, motivation and satisfaction of employees, developing high performance work culture, and achieving organizational goals.

The three compulsory ingredients of organizational DNA are: its mission (the purpose of organization's existence), the strategic direction (vision) where the organization is heading for, and organizational values.

The mission of the organization always gives answer for the question: why we exist in this world? The purpose of business goes much beyond the profit motives. It expands the organizational services to whole society. It also makes organization responsible to preserve the globe for life. Since the business organization does business within the society on this planet and utilizes its resources to generate wealth hence, it becomes the moral responsibility of the organization to share its wealth for the development of the society. This moral responsibility must reflect in the mission of the organization.

The strategic direction is an effective tool to streamline people to move together towards common destination. Vision is created by leaders by looking within, looking around and looking between the horizons.

Since organization is a collection of individuals who come from different backgrounds (cultures, social systems, social class, and families) having different perceptions and values, and in the absence of common guiding organizational values people try to impose their individual set of viewpoints on the organization. This situation set the core foundation for organizational conflicts. Therefore, it is imperative to have organizational values that can guide the needed behaviour of employees. These common organizational values are the main source to generate ethical organizational behaviour, sense of ownership, sense of contribution, sense of achievement, sense of humility, sense of service, proactivity, and sense of excellence among the people of the organization.

The leaders of top level are initially involved in developing the DNA of the organization and then utilize various human practices to generate people's commitment with the organizational DNA. Employees' commitment with organizational DNA produces enormous psychological energy needed to produce prodigious performances.

5

Leadership Styles

All the approaches and behaviours used by managers to influence others are elements of the managers' leadership style. Managers' leadership styles are composed of their use of power in how they choose to motivate, in their choice of decision making styles, in their choice of task or people orientation in the work environment.

Positive or Negative Motivation

Depending on the style of the manager, the motivation can take the form of rewards or penalties. As shown in Table 5.1, the positive leadership style deals in praise and recognition, monetary rewards, increase of security, and additional responsibility. This leadership style encourages development of employees through the creation of higher job satisfaction.

Penalties, loss of job, suspension, and public reprimands are extremes of negative leadership. This leadership style is based on threats and environment of fear.

TABLE 5.1 Positive and Negative Motivation Styles

Positive Motivation	*Negative Motivation*
Responsibility	Threats
Recognition	Coercion
Praise	Fines
Security	Suspension
Monitory rewards	Termination

Decision-making Style

The leaders basically follow three kinds of styles for making decision depending on the employees' educational status and complexity of decisions. These three kinds of styles are mentioned here:

Autocratic leadership style

This style describes decision making solely by the leaders with little or no flexibility of employees involvement. This style is preferable when the employees are not educated or competent enough to make correct decisions and/or the decision has serious impact on organization's survival. Majority of managers in the corporate world use this style because they do not trust their employees' competencies. With the result they make their employees passive followers.

The participative leadership style

This style is characterized by the leaders' involving the subordinates in the decision. The leaders who follow this style believe on "no involvement no commitment".

The free-rein style of leadership

This style is characterized by the leader's encouragement to individual or group to function independently. The leader either sets limits and the followers work out their own problems, or individuals set their own goals.

The participative and free-rein leadership styles require lots of ground work in terms of aligning people with the organizational DNA, teaching and mentoring them to understand environmental complexities, and to develop conceptual skills needed for good decision-making. Managers who do not have time and patience to do this ground work fall back to autocratic leadership style or use participative style in autocratic manner.

Task Orientation and Employee Orientation

Task orientation places emphasize on getting the job done through better methods, better control systems, assigning and organizing work, one person decision making, and monitoring through evaluation of performance. An employee oriented place on the other hand emphasizes on concern for the human needs of subordinates. They concentrate on teamwork, positive relationships, mutual respect, and solution to employees' problems.

Situational Leadership

Situational leadership concept is based on the assumption that there may not be universal leadership traits or single leadership behaviour and style applicable in all situations. The behaviour effective in some circumstances may be ineffective under different conditions. Thus, the effectiveness of a leader's behaviour is contingent upon organizational situations. As shown in Figure 6.1, the contingency approaches look for describing characteristics of situations and followers and examine the leadership styles that can be used effectively in different situations. All the three dimensions (leader, follower, and situation) shown in the situational model (Figure 6.1) need to be defined in detail to generate different leadership styles suitable in different situations.

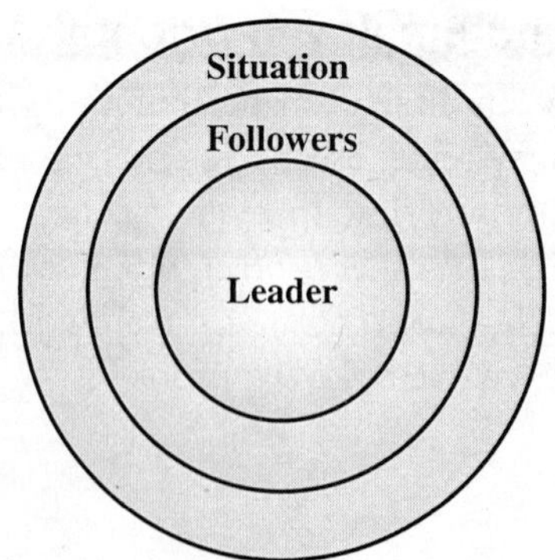

Figure 6.1 Situational leadership.

SITUATIONAL LEADERS

A good situational leader is one who can quickly change leadership styles as the situation changes. Following are the parameters on which situational leaders must concentrate and achieve mastry to adopt best suited styles in different circumstances.

Characteristics of Situational Leaders

Integrated human being

As an integrated human being leaders should possess right mix of physical, mental and emotional acumen. The physical acumen is needed to maintain healthy body, the mental acumen develops analytical and creative brain, and the emotional acumen provides emotional control and humility. These dimensions of integrated human being are defined and discussed in detail in Section II of this book. The right mix of all types of acumen is extremely important to become a role model, win people's trust and confidence, and to sustain long-term relationships with them. No leader can survive for long period by just using external appearance and manipulative techniques.

Transformational leaders

Leaders must follow transformational approach and become a transformational leader. Transformational leaders work from the root and are involved in developing followers into leaders. They bring productive changes in the organization so that the organization can sail safely in turbulant environment.

Leadership behaviour

The behaviour of leaders dwell on task and people continuum. They require keeping balance in their *task-oriented* and *people-oriented behaviour*. Both necessary to run the organization effectively.

Leadership styles

The path-goal theory (House and Mitchell 1974) suggests the fourfold classification of a leader's behaviour. These four types of behaviours include supportive, directive, achievement-oriented, and participative style.

1. The **Supportive** leadership shows concern for subordinates' needs and well-being. Leadership behaviour is open, friendly and approachable.
2. **Directive** leadership tells subordinates exactly what they are supposed to do. They are involved in planning, making scheduling, and setting performance goals.

3. **Achievement-oriented** leadership sets clear and challenging tasks and stresses on high quality performances. They show confidence over their subordinates' capabilities.
4. **Participative** leadership involved subordinates in making the decisions. The leaders involve subordinates to give their suggestions and opinions in making decisions.

Hersey and Blanchard's situational theory (1988) suggests four styles of leadership that can be used in different situations. The four styles are telling, selling, participating and delegating.

1. **Telling** is a very directive style. It involves giving explicit direction about how the tasks should be accomplished.
2. **Selling** involves providing direction, but also includes seeking inputs from others before making decisions.
3. Under **delegating** style the employees assume responsibility for their work and for the success of their organization.
4. Participative style is already described above.

The contingency model (Vroom and Jago 1988) compiled five levels of leaders' participative decision-making styles ranging from highly autocratic to highly democratic. The employees' involvement in decision-making is increasing from autocratic (participation almost none) to democratic (maximum participation) style.

FOLLOWERS

If a leader does not have any follower then he/she is simply walking alone on a street. It is the followers who decide about the good or bad leadership. We can consider ourself as a good leader only if our followers want to follow us next time.

In a position of leadership, an individual is influenced by his relationship with followers and also by actions and attitudes of followers. Hersey and Blanchard (1988) suggested that the appropriate leadership style depends on the development or readiness of followers. They categorize followers' readiness into four categories from R1 to R4. R1 is low readiness of followers where followers are unable and unwilling to take the responsibility of their own task. In R2, the followers are willing to take the task but unable to do the task. R3 category followers are actually able but unwilling to take the responsibility and in R4, the followers are able and also willing to take up the responsibility. The grid for all the four followers' readiness categories is shown in Table 6.1.

TABLE 6.1 Followers' Readiness

	Unwilling	*Willing*
Able	R3	R4
Unable	R1	R2

Followership Patterns

There are basically five types of followership patterns. In the Figure 6.2, the followership patterns are categorized according to two dimensions. The first dimension is high mental acumen versus low mental acumen. Persons with high mental acumen are aware of the importance of the actions of their own and others. They can make good decisions. They can do creative criticism, and bring innovative ideas. On the other hand, the person with low mental acumen does not contribute to cultivation of the organization, and accepts the leaders' ideas without thinking. The second dimension is proactive versus reactive focus. The proactive followers participate willingly in the work and take responsibility beyond their job. Conversely reactive followers need constant supervision and control, and do not want to take responsibility beyond what is given by leaders.

The extent to which one is proactive and reactive and with high and low mental acumen determines whether followers are estranged, inactive, conformist, situational manipulator, or a valuable follower (Figure 6.2).

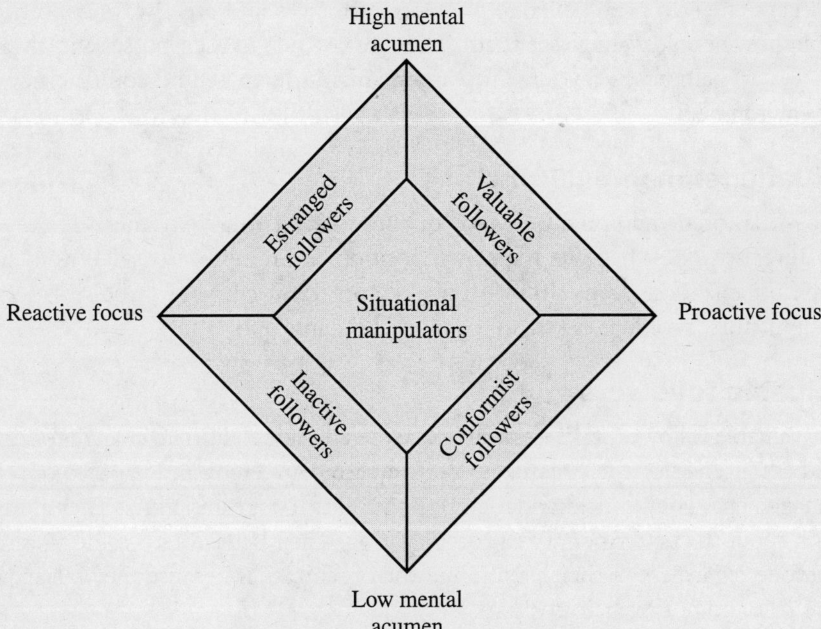

Figure 6.2 Followership diamond.

Estranged followers

The estranged followers are reactive but yet having high mental acumen. They are capable but they do not participate in developing solutions to the problems or deficiencies they observe in the organization. They focus more on others' affaires and organizational shortcomings. They are emotionally week and always guided by external forces. They form their own group within the organization and try to put hurdles on others' way and search for opportunities to put their opponent group down by highlighting their weaknesses.

Inactive followers

Inactive followers' activity is limited to what they are told to do, and they accomplish things only with a great deal of supervision. They do not want to take initiatives, do not understand their responsibility to find solutions for existing problem. They are change resisters and always want to be in their comfort zone. They do the work for the sake of doing and not for generating excellence. They are often the result of leaders who are over controlling others and punish mistakes.

Conformist followers

The conformist followers participate actively in the organizational activities but do not utilize mental acumen in their task behaviour. They do whatever they are asked to do without thinking about consequences because they want to avoid conflict. They do not challenge poor performances and are always concerned about how people want to see them. They are yes men to their bosses and always say 'yes' to gain boss's favour. They are the main source behind complacency in the environment.

Situational manipulators

The situational manipulators have qualities of all four extremes. They use whatever style best benefits their own position and minimizes risk. Within any given organization, some 30 to 40 per cent of followers tend to be situational manipulators, avoiding risks and fostering the status quo.

Valuable followers

The valuable followers take risks and have the courage to initiate change to serve the best interest of the organization. They are competent and capable of self-management. They understand their responsibility to take initiatives. They always think about the betterment of the organization. Their behaviour is same towards everyone regardless of their position in the organization because they believe in their role and not in their position.

WHAT FOLLOWERS EXPECT FROM A LEADER?

The followers are looking for four main characteristics in leaders: honesty, competence, forward looking, and inspiring.

Honesty

Honesty comprises doing what a person says he/she is going to do, consistency between word and deed, displaying trust in others, and taking stand on important principles and beliefs.

Competence

A persons' competence is seen as his/her capability and effectiveness, adding value to the team and creating difference with his/her presence in the organization, abilities to challenge and inspire, and also being enable to model the way.

Forward Looking

A person is forward looking when he/she has a clear set of directions, knows where to go and provides direction through vision and goals.

Inspiring

A person can be inspiring by inducing enthusiasm and energy in his/her followers, giving them positive picture about their future, and displaying passion for the cause.

LEADERSHIP SITUATION

The Fiedler's model (Fiedler 1972) presents the leadership situation in terms of three key elements: the quality of leader-members relations, task structure, and position power.

Leader-members Relations

When subordinates trust, respect, and have confidence in their leader, the leader-members relations are considered as good. When subordinates distrust, do not respect, and have little confidence in the leader, leader-members relations are poor.

Task Structure

Routine, well defined tasks such as those of assembly line workers have high degree of structure. Creative ill defined tasks such as research and development, strategic planning, have low degree of task structure. The high task structure is considered as favourable to leaders and the low task structure is unfavourable.

Position Power

Position power is high when the leader has the power to plan and direct the work of subordinates, evaluate it, and reward or punish them. Position power is low when the leader has little authority over subordinates, and cannot evaluate their work or reward them. When position power is high, the situation is favourable and when the position power is low, the situation is unfavourable for leaders.

Along with the Fiedler's situational elements, path-goal theory (House and Mitchell, 1974) suggest another situational element that is work-group characteristics which includes their educational levels and quality of relationship among them.

WHAT SHOULD BE AN APPROPRIATE STYLE OF LEADERSHIP?

Finally the question arises that what should be the leaders' approach in different types of situations. As a leader in any situation, one should first deeply explore all the three dimensions of situational leadership: leader, follower and situation. After the deep exploration you can find out the areas needing improvement in long-run and what kind of leadership style is required to control the situation and improve the performance in short-run. Thus, the two important leadership approaches are required in any situation: long-run improvement and short-term controlling.

In short-term controlling one can use appropriate leadership style according to followers and situations. A persons' style may range from highly autocratic to highly democratic, positive motivation to negative motivation, and task-oriented behaviour to employee-oriented behaviour.

But the core focus should be on long-run improvement and that is a job of transformational leader. It is needed to first ensure that a person is an integrated human being and has all the effective characteristics that an effective leader requires. Through the mentoring, teaching and coaching skills, effective leadership traits and behaviour, the development of followers into effective followers is done, who are proactive and have high physical, mental and emotional acumen. Remember, the leaders generate their power not from position but from their followers, therefore, it is needed to develop synergistic agreement and trustful relationship with ones followers so that the followers trust, respect, and have confidence in the leader. To improve the situation it is needed to improve working environment by developing effective work culture. Learning attitude in the organizational environment is extremely vital. Both leaders and followers need to show the humility of admitting that they do not have all the answers, and that everyone can make a meaningful contribution.

7

Transactional and Transformational Leadership

Transactional leadership places emphasis on the extrinsic relationship between leaders and followers. It examines the mutual benefit from an exchange-based relationship with the leader offering certain things, such as resources or rewards in return of others, such as the followers' commitment or acceptance of the leader's authority.

TRANSACTIONAL LEADERS

Transactional leaders guide or motivate their followers in the direction of established goals by clarifying role and task requirements. In fine we can say that transactional leaders:

- get normal people to complete routine job successfully.
- clarify the needs of business and break them down into manageable objectives.
- evaluate the needs of staff and reward accordingly.
- are very effective for improving and maintaining performance.
- determine the abilities of staff and delegates accordingly.

TRANSFORMATIONAL LEADERS

In twenty first century the transformational leaders are those who stay ahead of the change curve, constantly redefining their industries, creating new markets, blazing new trails, reinventing the competitive rules, and challenging the status quo. They achieve these tasks through looking forward, scanning the landscape, watching the competition, spotting the emerging trends and new opportunities, and avoiding future crisis. They have a vision, a passion, and an exciting aspiration. They share this aspiration with everybody in the organization to unleash tremendous psychological energy. This psychological energy provides the fuel to push organization out of its competitors.

Transformational leaders are involved in developing followers into leaders through modelling, mentoring, teaching and empowerment. They provide high self-esteem to their followers.

They create vision first and then streamline diverse group of people with it in the organization. They use vision as a tool to pull people and to provide common direction to them. They bring people from denial stage to commitment stage; empower them to take initiatives and decisions. They encourage their employees to participate in the development of organizational mission, and make sure that each employee is the stakeholder of the mission.

Transformational leaders pay attention to each individual's need for growth and development. They motivate and inspire employees intrinsically; recognize their performances, give rewards and celebrate their small wins. They instigate people to do more than what is expected and advocate them to go extra mile.

Transformational Leaders Possess Charisma

"Charisma" in leaders is defined as being attributed with extraordinary personal characteristics like:

- Self-confidence
- Strong convictions of the rightness of their beliefs
- Persistence
- Flexibility
- Energy/enthusiasm
- Risk-taking ability
- Confidence in others' capabilities

Charismatic leaders do not demand attention, they command it. They provide vision and sense of mission, instil pride, gain respect and trust.

Key Characteristics of Charismatic Leader

Envisioning

They have a vision which is expressed as an idealized goal, that proposes a future better than the status quo. They are able to clarify the importance of the vision in terms that are understandable to others. They are set high expectation and model consistent behaviour.

Energizing

They demonstrate personal excitement and express personal confidence; seek, find, and use success.

Enabling

They empathize, express confidence in people, and express personal support. They are perceptive of followers' abilities and responsive to their needs and feelings.

Personal risk

They are willing to take on high personal risks, engage in self-sacrifice to achieve the vision.

Environment sensitivity

Able to make realistic assessments of the environmental constraints and resources needed to bring about changes.

WHAT DO CHARISMATIC LEADERS DO?

- Have a remarkable ability to distill complex ideas into simple messages.
- Communicate by using symbols, analogies, metaphors and stories.
- Lead people ahead.
- Relish risk and feel empty without it.
- Great optimists.
- Rebels who fight convention.
- Inspire and create excitement among people of the organization.
- Galvanize people into action.

FOUR POWERS OF TRANSFORMATIONAL LEADERS

The four powers of transformational leaders are presence, intention, wisdom and compassion.

They are always present in the environment like aroma of delicious food, peace of monasteries, and fragrance of incense sticks. Their ambition, aspirations, and vision constantly guide and energize the people in the organization. They tirelessly perform their role of mentorship and stewardship to take care of everyone in the organization.

Their intentions are divine as they do their job without any expectations. They are passionate to sacrifice for others, focused on organizational goals, loyal to their people, faithful to their ethical values, and committed to organizational DNA.

Their wisdom helps them to keep sense of balance, control their emotions, and to utilize their knowledge and skills fruitfully for the organizational development.

They are compassionate to people. They are empathetic to their subordinates and want to understand their emotions and afflictions. They are exuberant, creative, spontaneous, and use their brain sometime, but heart all the time.

Leadership Behaviour at Workplace

A series of studies at Ohio State University (Stogdill and Coons 1957) identified two leadership dimensions that accounted 85 per cent of the variance in description of leadership behaviour: initiating structure and consideration. Initiating structure is the degree to which a leader organizes relationships in the group by assigning specific tasks, specifying procedures to be followed, scheduling work, and clarifying expectations of team members.

Some self-assessment items measuring initiating structure are as follows:

1. Implementation of innovative ideas in the work group.
2. Great emphasis on beating the deadlines.
3. Encourage the lethargic workers to work harder to improve productivity.
4. Regular group meetings.
5. Ensuring that people are working to their fullest capacity.

Consideration is the degree to which the leader creates an environment of emotional support, warmth, friendliness, trust and concentrate on aligning all the stakeholders of the organization. The leader creates this environment by being friendly and approachable, looking out for the personal welfare of the group, and doing small favours for the group.

Some self-assessment items measuring considerations done by a leader are as follows:

1. Does personal favours for people in the work group.

2. Treats all people in the work group equal.
3. Is always ready to bring relevant changes.
4. Cooperates to the group members.
5. Shows little courtesies to the group members.

At the same time a researcher of Survey Research Centre, University of Michigan, made the study on leadership effectiveness in the organization and developed two approaches to leadership. In findings supervisory leaders were categorized into two groups, depending on whether they emphasized production or employees. Production-centred leaders set tight work standards, organized tasks carefully, and prescribed the work methods to be followed. Employee-centred leaders encouraged subordinate's participation in goal setting and in other work decisions. They also helped to ensure high performance by engendering mutual trust and respect.

An important implication from both the studies is that effective leaders emphasize both high productivity and good interpersonal relationships. In almost all the leadership situations it is needed to keep balance in the leadership behaviour between two dimensions of **task orientation** and **people orientation** as shown in Figure 8.1.

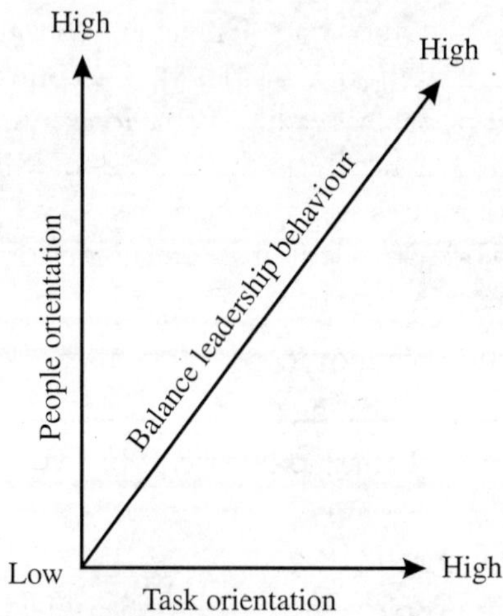

Figure 8.1 Balance leadership behaviour between task and people orientation.

TASK ORIENTED LEADERSHIP BEHAVIOUR

The task oriented behaviour of leaders focuses on the task to be performed than on the interpersonal aspect of leadership. Different task oriented behaviours of leaders are as follows:

Adaptability to the situation

Effective leaders adapt to the situation according to the given position, power, relationship with people and maturity level of the relationship with people. A leader chooses the tactics best suited for a particular situation. The adaptive leader also selects an organizational structure best suited to the demands of the situation. The ability to size up people and situations, and adapt tactics accordingly is a vital leadership behaviour. It stems from insight and intuition, both of which reflect a talent for direct perception of a situation, unrelated to any specific reasoning process.

Envisioning

Kotter (1996) reasons that since the leadership is involved in producing change, the leader must set the direction of that change. Setting direction goes beyond planning as planning is more deductive based on set rules and existing knowledge. Setting direction is more inductive and requires the gathering of voluminous data and search for patterns, relationships, and linkages that help to explain events. Direction setting creates vision and strategies rather than a plan. In turn, the vision describes a business, technology or corporate culture in terms of what it should become. The strategy describes a feasible way of achieving the vision.

High performance standards

Effective leaders consistently hold group members to high standards of performance. Setting such standards increase productivity, as people tend to live up to the expectations set for them by superiors. Leaders are also concern to raise performance standard at workplace by focusing on results, adding value, establishing partnerships and taking systemic view.

Risk taking and willingness to take action

Combined with risk taking, willingness to take action is also very important task-oriented leadership behaviour. To bring about constructive change as a leader it is must to take risk and be willing to implement the risky decisions. Following are the characteristics of risk-taker and action believer given by DuBrin (1995):

- Willing to take personal risks to advance new ideas and programmes for the success of the company.
- Has the courage to commit sizeable resources based on a blend of analysis and intuition.
- Is comfortable with making the percentages rather than achieving success with each initiative.
- Trusts own judgement and instincts without requiring definitive proof.
- Prefer quick and approximate actions to slow and precise approaches.
- By taking risk and implementing changes in the system leaders perform their role as a change agent.

Environmental interpretation

Leaders are engaged in interpreting internal and external conditions that affect the leader and the organizational unit. Leader is involved in carrying out the management role of environmental sensing. When significant trends are observed, the leader helps the group to develop an action plan to capitalize on or defend against the trends.

Providing feedback

Providing regular and frequent feedback to group members is a vital task behaviour of a leader. By giving performance feedback a leader influence the actions of his/her group members. Feedback of this nature has two aspects: First, group members are informed how well they are doing so they can take corrective action if needed. Second, positive feedback serves as a motivator that prompts group members to continue constructive activities.

Customer focus

Effective leaders are strongly interested in satisfying the needs of the customers, clients, or constituents; this approach helps to inspire employees to satisfy customers.

RELATIONSHIP ORIENTED LEADERSHIP BEHAVIOUR

Leadership involves in building relationship with people, so it follows that many effective leadership attitudes, behaviours and practices deal with interpersonal relationships.

Alignment of people

According to Kotter (1996), aligning people is more of a communication's challenge than a problem of organizing. To pull people and align them with organization's vision, mission, and strategies, it is extremely important to talk to more people and encourage the two way communication. Quite simply, leaders endear themselves to stakeholders by bringing the interests of all stakeholder groups into strategic alignment. No stakeholder group benefits at the expense of any other stakeholder group, and each prospers as the others do. Leaders use their vision as an important tool to align people towards same direction.

Mobilization

Whereas alignment of people takes place at emotional level, mobilization is more involved with getting the group working together smoothly. Mobilizing practices include:

- Clarifying each other's expectations.
- Generating people's commitment towards common mission and goals.
- Developing mutual responsibility and accountability.
- Demonstrating confidence in the abilities of others.
- Letting people know how they are progressing towards the group's goal.

Harmonizing

Through aligning, mobilizing, and synchronizing everyone's job, leaders create harmony in the organization. The system can be thought of as a large modern orchestra with a number of professionals playing quite different instruments and performing separate tasks. Each instrumentalist is indeed a specialist in a particular instrument whose performance must be integrated with the performances of others to make up the whole and create harmony.

Mentoring

In a mentor's role, the transformational leader clearly identifies the potentials that are in dormant state in the employees and the critical areas needing work. He provides personalized training as a teacher, counsellor, and coach to his employees to develop their potentials to the maximum.

Inspiration

Inspiring others is an essential leadership practice. Following are some inspiring practices:

- Promoting the development of people's talents.
- Recognizing the contribution of others.
- Enabling others to feel like leaders.
- Stimulating other's thinking.
- Building enthusiasm about projects and assignments.

Satisfaction of human needs

To inspire people, effective leaders motivate people by satisfying higher level needs like needs for achievement, a sense of belonging, recognition, and self-esteem, etc.

Emotional support

Supportive behaviour towards team members usually increases leadership effectiveness. A supportive leader gives frequent encouragement and praise. The emotional support improves morale of the people.

9

Leadership in Indian Culture

In the case of India, the national culture has evolved into a hybrid approach towards leadership practices. India is rooted in a framework of transcendent ideology, as a result the primary mode of behaviour is supported by traditional approach, as well as secondary mode is supported by western influence. This leads to a unique superior-subordinate relationships, work behaviour and leadership practices. Westernization of Indian firms has significant impact on leadership practices of their executives.

American sales persons are socialized in a culture characterized by low power-distance and high degree of individualism. They dislike authority, conformity and closed supervision.

Sales persons of Indian origin are raised in an environment emphasizing high degrees of collective dependence and power-distance and respond favourably to tighter control and supervision. This means Indian workers prefer authoritative and hierarchical forms of management. Bosses are expected to demonstrate powerful personalities. Leaders who demonstrate high power type of behaviour are more likely to gain the respect of subordinates. Clear and direct orders are preferred. The lack of clear job descriptions and expectations, fluid timeframes, or ambiguity in job objectives negatively affect the work behaviour of Indian workers.

Indian employees value good relationships between superior and subordinates. Such relationships are highly power-based, with leaders as power figures. The western style leaders on the other hand place highest importance on driving the workforce towards developing self initiative, creativity and entrepreneurship in their jobs. Indian workers may view the democratic management styles adopted by leaders as a sign of weakness or incompetence.

American employees generally have internal locus of control and because of this the responsibility and accountability lie with the individual and outcomes cannot be shifted to an unknown supernatural force. The traditional culture of India socializes people to be predisposed towards an external locus of control. They believe that humankind is basically helpless in influencing life's events which are largely controlled by fate and supernatural forces.

The managers and other professionals from India working in developed world are able to have high level of achievement not only because of access to superior resources but also because of the prevailing mindset that encourages and nurtures an internal locus of control.

Indian organizations have invested considerable resources, time and effort to adopt state-of-the-art human resource management practices developed in Europe and North America. While the poor leadership practices, bureaucratic inefficiencies and low productivity evident in many organizations creates pressure to adopt quick solutions, the effectiveness of this approach is open to serious questions.

There are many unresolved questions regarding the models of management that can be adapted to Indian context, such as what sort of example of management are we setting? Can it be transferred from one economy to another? Are its policies and practices internationally applicable? All these questions many a times have disturbed many formally accepted concepts specially those relating to management of people.

Most of the management concepts in developing countries like India have been borrowed from the West. During the last three decades the western especially the American concepts of management have become popular in India and to a large extent efforts are made to absorb some of these concepts in wide variety of organizational settings. The concepts ranged from the scientific management, management by objective to emphasize on business process reengineering, etc.

Modelled on the western education, Indian universities and institutes have formulated courses in management to meet the demands for qualified managerial personnel. Similarly, consultants suggest restructuring of the organization and systems based on the western models. Thus, today an Indian manager is educated either in the west or trained in western management literature attempts to manage and administer the Indian industrial structure on western principles. This, the manager finds, does not work. Compromises results, often accompanied by frustration. Interestingly, work does proceed and goals are to an extent achieved. Management is "somehow" affected.

Because of these reasons, the leadership in India is characterized by having double standards. There is distinct unconformity between what is taught and written as policies and the actual leadership practices followed by Indian managers. The cultural learning dominate on what is taught in management courses and Indian manager follows power-distance from employees, consider themselves as a person with more knowledge and of higher status, concerned with their image in society and how they are perceived among their employees. They believe that if they will become democratic then they would be perceived as weak leaders. They try to be rude to project themselves as strong leaders. They are reluctant to change because of impact of traditions on their behaviour. They follow participative leadership style in autocratic manner, means they allow their employees to participate in decision-making, but impose their own thinking and decisions only, or embrace employee's decision only when it is in commensuration with their own thought.

WHAT SHOULD BE THE APPROPRIATE LEADERSHIP STYLE IN INDIAN CULTURE?

In Indian culture, leaders must follow the two-layer leadership style as described in Chapter 7 of situational leadership. In one surface layer style, leaders should concentrate on short-term hierarchical controlling, ranging from close supervision, right mix of autocratic and participative approach, management by objectives, and balanced power-distance with task and people consideration. On the other hand, at deeper layer leaders should concentrate on long-term transformation and perform their role as mentor and change agent. They should make efforts on their followers' development ranging from internal locus of control, management knowledge and skills, decision-making capability, empowerment, and critical thinking. Also, they should develop appropriate work environment and high-performance divine culture.

10

World-class Organization

All the organizations are striving for world-class leaders to transform average performance into world-class performance. The world-class performance is the ultimate competitiveness strategy for organizations entering the new millennium. Can Indian companies meet the challenge? The world-class organizations create real wealth for stakeholders through meeting their expectations.

They provide consistent and long-term returns on investments of shareholders, equitable remuneration, development, and learning opportunities to their employees, superior quality of products and services at low cost to their customers, adhere to society norms and values. They also contribute largely in developing earth as sweet home for mankind through environmental preservation. They meet these demands by "doing the right things right". World-class companies are striving first and foremost for effectiveness (doing the right thing) and then efficiency (doing things right).

To create world-class organization, it is needed to find the answer to following questions:

- What are the attributes of a world-class organization?
- What are the need categories of the world-class organizations?
- What is a high performance organization?

ATTRIBUTES OF WORLD-CLASS ORGANIZATIONS

These organizations are unique in terms of products, services, corporate culture, and people. Through their unique and effective work culture they focus on converting their resources into competences and develop core competences which cannot be imitated by competitors. They are high performance organizations and are global players that have the capabilities to compete on opposition's home turf. They quickly detect and respond to changing business environment. They are innovation-driven and see their employees as an asset on balance sheet, not cost element on income statement. They have corruption-free and fair labour practices and are sensitive to environmental issues. They understand their responsibility and feel themselves accountable for the protection of environment.

Raj Sisodia, Jag Sheth and David B. Wolfe in their book *Firms of Endearment* (2007), have mentioned that the world-class organizations are actually the endearing organizations. According to them a "firm of endearment" is a company that endears itself to stakeholders by bringing the interests of all stakeholder groups into strategic alignment. No stakeholder group benefits at the expense of any other stakeholder group, and each prospers as the others do. These FoEs meet the tangible and intangible needs of their stakeholders in ways that delight them and engender affection for loyalty to company. FoEs have brought into a different idea; they strive for *share of heart* rather than *share of wallet*. Earn a share of customers' heart and they will gladly offer you bigger share of their wallet. Do the same for an employee and the employee will give back with a quantum leap in productivity and work quality. Emotionally bond with your suppliers, and reap the benefits of superiors' offerings and responsiveness. Give communities in which you operate reasons to feel pride in your presence, and enjoy a fertile source of customers and employees.

Figure 10.1 shows the strategic alignment of the firm with all its stakeholders, society—the ultimate stakeholder, and environment where all are benefited with the firm's existence and are involved in protecting the environment.

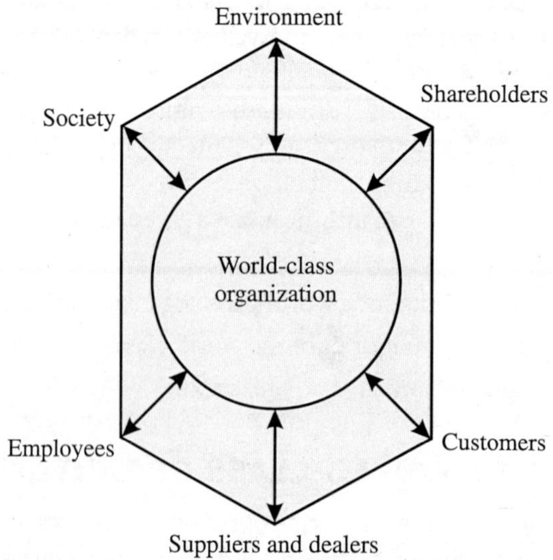

Figure 10.1 Strategic alignments of a firm.

Many world-class organizations have special environmental mission statements to guide their operations. For example, Starbucks lists seven principles in its environmental mission statement, which is as follows:

1. Understanding environmental issues and sharing information with our partners.
2. Developing innovative and flexible solutions to bring about change.
3. Striving to buy, sell, and use environment friendly products.
4. Recognizing that fiscal responsibility is essential to our environmental future.
5. Instilling environmental responsibility as a corporate value.
6. Measuring and monitoring our progress for each project.
7. Encouraging all partners to share in our mission.

WORLD-CLASS ORGANIZATIONS' NEEDS

Just like human needs there are organizational needs that have to be fulfilled by all the employees of the organization. Table 10.1 shows three categories of needs of world-class organization that are subsistence, association and escalation needs. An organization that successfully achieves these needs can become a world-class organization.

From Table 10.1, it is evident that an organization cannot become world-class only by merely capturing the highest market share, market capitalization, and achieving all types of subsistence and association needs. The level of achievement on escalation needs decides the title of being world-class. Ryuzaburo (1997) visionary president and later chairman of Canon challenged the leaders of large global corporations with this thought:

> *"Because multibillion-dollar corporations control vast resources around the globe, employ millions of people, create and own incredible wealth, and they hold the future of the planet in their hands. Although governments and individuals need to do their part, they do not possess the same degree of wealth and power. If corporations run their businesses with the sole aim of gaining more market share or earning more profits, they may well lead the world into economic, environmental and social ruin. It is our obligation as business leaders to join together to build a foundation for world peace and prosperity".*

Though the organizations unable to satisfy their subsistence and association needs effectively may not really satisfy escalation needs in terms of effectiveness. Therefore, it is essential to become a high performance organization first.

TABLE 10.1 Organizational Needs

Organizational Need Categories	*Need Examples*
Escalation needs	• Corporate social responsibility, • Global economic wealth creation, • Acting as role model for human values, • Invention and adoption of environment-friendly technologies to save planet, • Recycling of own products, • Creating income balance between developed, developing and underdeveloped countries, • Corporate-government partnership for finding innovative solutions to diverse problems, • Wealth-sharing with weakest sections of the society. Bringing peace and harmony in society.
Association needs	• Need for collaboration and partnership with organization's community like suppliers, dealers, and customers, • Need for competitors, social organizations and various academic institutions to enhance knowledge and skills.
Subsistence needs	• Developing strong market share, • Consolidate companies position in the market, • TQM, • Profit optimization, • Management and employee relationships, • Employees' development as integrated human beings, • Employee security, • Core competences' development, • Lower employee turnover, etc.

HIGH PERFORMING WORLD-CLASS ORGANIZATIONS

"We understand that the company with the ability to learn and to act on that learning faster than anyone else, has the ultimate competitive advantage. If we let our people flourish and grow, if we use the best ideas they come up with, then we have a chance to win.

Jack Welch (2001)

The high performance organizations are responsive organizations where there is proper alignment of people, process and technology and share the wealth equitably with all stakeholders and society as a whole. They develop in much faster pace than their competitions and sustain their rates. In high performance organizations all the stakeholders and processes come first and technology is in supporting role.

The five important components of high performance organizations are employee involvement, self directing work teams, integrated production technology, learning organization, and total quality management (Schermerhorn, Osborn, and Hunt 2003). Other important components of high performance organization are high-performance divine culture, creative human resource management, society based focus and open climate.

Employee Involvement

In the high performing organizations, the employees are committed to organizational vision, mission and values (DNA). They are also committed to each other and this commitment goes much beyond organizational boundaries to personal level with very strong emotional bonds. Employees are also fully committed to extend their services to the stakeholders without any expectations of future gains and rewards.

Self Directing Teams

A team is a small number of people with complementary skills who are committed to a common purpose, performance goals, and approach for which they hold themselves mutually accountable (Katzenbach and Smith 2006).

Self directing work teams are empowered to make decisions about key aspects of their individual work. They have common approach and the leadership role is rotated among the team members.

Integrated Production Technology

Integrated production technologies focus on providing flexibility in manufacturing and services and involve job design and information systems as a part of technology (Schermerhorn et al. 2003). The world-class organizations are always involved in developing and adopting new eco-friendly technologies. They have most modern and effective information systems. They have the technology to recycle their products.

Learning Organizations

Learning organizations scan the environment, anticipate changing trends, and develop and embrace new technologies much faster than the competition. They have proactive approach towards learning new dimensions and consider learning as valuable tool to improve organizational performance.

The organization is continuously involved in benchmarking, empowering their employees, developing innovation based reward systems for their employees. According to changing needs world-class organizations go for outsourcing, rightsizing, and business process reengineering.

Total Quality Management

Total Quality Management (TQM) is dedicated to ensure that an organization is committed to high quality, continuous improvement, and customer satisfaction. Quality in this sense means that customer's needs are met and that all tasks are executed correctly at the first time. These attributes and characteristics lead to outstanding performance in market standing, employee enthusiasm, customer response, innovation, productivity, quality and profitability.

High-performance Gracious Culture

High-performance companies consider corporate culture as secret weapon to win the competition. High-performance gracious culture brings out the best in people. It is a kind of fertile soil that grows competences, core competences and excellence. The gracious culture is defined in detail in Chapter 29.

Creative Human Resource Management

In the High-performing world-class organization the HR people know the saying "our people are our greatest assets", but do not consider it as a slogan only to put it in an annual report or to write it on the company's wall, rather they consider it as bottom line reality. You cannot provide exceptional services, achieve innovative breakthroughs, or respond rapidly to marketplace changes with an unmotivated, over burdened or burnt out workforce. Developing high-performance culture is always in the HR department's short list of key result areas. The effective training programs are organized constantly for the development of employees. The employees are constantly mentored to attain mode of graciousness. The relationship between initiative and rewards, and performance and reward is clearly understood by employees. Employees are constantly motivated to take initiatives and to pursue the rewards. Recognition is given openly and is publicized throughout the organization.

Society Based Focus

For high performing world-class organization, society is ultimate stakeholder. The organization's structure, processes and tasks are designed to serve the society.

The information systems ensure prompt response to changing needs of the people. The compensations are designed to reward employees for excellent service.

Open Climate

In the climate of high performing world-class organizations there exists open communication, strong business ethics, environment-friendly systems, employee participation, wellness and family programs. Leaders are involved in mentoring and coaching of their subordinates. They provide all the information to their employees and other stakeholders in order to make the organization transparent.

11

Strategic Leadership Cycle

There is no finishing line for leadership and organizational development. Best leaders are always preparing for tomorrow. Every moment the environment is changing, therefore, today's success becomes tomorrow's status quo. In the same manner new business portfolios that are profitable in the present and are considered as factors for organizational growth, become burden to organization in future and contribute intensively in making the organization overweight. In this constantly changing environment there are four strategic leadership roles needed to be performed at different stages of organizational development. These strategic leadership roles are being risk-taker, caretaker, surgeon, and undertaker (Rothschild 1993).

In risk-taker role, a person has to be visionary, missionary, and innovator. It is needed to develop the organization on the person's own dream. He/she has to explore systems within the organization and see its workability in the environment by looking around and beyond the horizons. With the help of this analysis and his/her intuitive skills a person can add different portfolios that can provide growth to his/her organization.

Once the organization start sailing on new path and direction with various portfolios, he/she can switch over his/her role as caretaker to institutionalize the system so that company grows profitably, perhaps for decades. The caretaker works within the organizational paradigm and creates order to increase productivity with the help of proper planning, organizing, directing and controlling functions. Different businesses can be productive for various time periods depending on industry and product life cycles.

When the business becomes overweight, complacent and slow, and when some of the portfolios become the burden on the organization, it is time for the surgeon to take the command. Surgeon leaders are analytical, objective and freed from the past, nothing is sacred to them. They focus on the vital organs of the business and determine the most profitable way to remove the organs that lack strategic fit. They perform skilled surgery to cut out those organs.

After the successful surgery you need to undertake the organization to work as shock absorber against the surgical effects and to concentrate on future business development. Lots of patience is required to absorb these shocks.

SECTION II

LEADER AS INTEGRATED HUMAN BEING

12

Power of Leaders

Most people perceive themselves as powerless and feel that they are unable to make difference in their lives or in the world. This feeling of powerlessness leads our attention to the point of obsession means more money, more possessions, and more authority, etc. We think that if we can just get a bit more of that, we can control our lives and feel safe and secure. But the real power comes from within and those who generate power from their inner paradigm become charismatic or magnetic personalities. They impress not because they want to but because of the energy they radiate.

As shown in Figure 12.1, the power of leaders lies in their personal paradigm from where they generate their strengths, wisdom, and power to take actions.

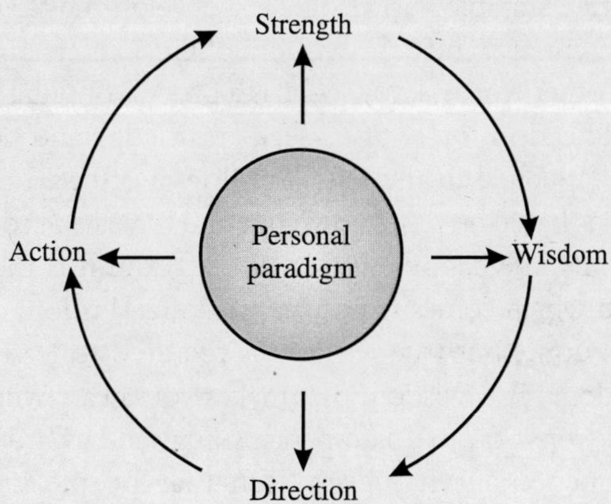

Figure 12.1 Power of leaders.

Many research observations have indicated that leaders have certain personality traits. They are always guided by their own set of rules and values and do not get affected by external forces. These characteristics contribute to leadership effectiveness in many situations as long as the leaders' style fits the situation reasonably well.

Strength represents our sense of worth, emotional anchorage and independency. It comes from our personal values, attitude, habits, self-esteem, knowledge, skills, competences, experiences, and internal locus of control.

Once Anna Freud said that, "I was looking outside myself for strength and confidence but it comes from within. It is there all the times". To achieve our dreams we have the strength within ourselves. That is the strength of character, which provides us ability to overcome resentment against others, to hide hurt feelings, and to forgive others' mistakes. We do not have any control over outside events but we can control our own mind and by doing this we generate the strength. Our actual strength comes from kindness, gentleness and tenacity. We should consider ourselves as steel not the glass because hammer forges the steel but shatter the glass. The depth of our strength may be defined from our moral reserves. Majority of people worship dead men for their strength, forgetting that they have the strength in themselves. The important thing about a problem is not its solution, but the strength we gain in finding the solution. To reclaim our strength, we need to let go our fears of making mistakes and leaving our comfort zone, stop worrying about what others think, and open ourselves to the constant flow of ideas, opportunities, and energies that are available to everyone of us, all the time.

Wisdom dwells on continuum of inaccuracy to accuracy in the perspective of life, and sense of balance. It is actually ability to apply your knowledge, competences, and values to take correct decisions in any situation. The function of wisdom is to discriminate between good and bad or right and wrong. Acquiring knowledge is no guarantee of practical useful application. Through our wisdom we integrate suitable knowledge and develop the talent to take out the essential from inessentials. Thus, the wisdom of life consists in the elimination of non-essentials. In other words, knowledge is a process of piling up facts; wisdom lies in their simplification. Most of us seek knowledge and not wisdom. If we know that what happened in the past and how it affected the situation, it is knowledge, which is based on past knowledge and if we want to predict the future events, it is wisdom. The happy mind is true wisdom it is the supreme part of happiness in mind which comes from true wisdom. Wisdom definitely requires for getting things done, but true wisdom is required to learn the noble art of leaving things undone. It is wisdom that makes you aware when to be generous and when firm. It stops you to do desperate things and award you the power to anticipate consequences. It has been seen that people having remarkable education and knowledge failed in their endeavours because of lack of common sense. Wisdom is one's common sense. It is better to have wisdom without education than to have education without wisdom. If you get a chance to keep your mouth shut, do not pass a chance to others because the first step to wisdom is silence; the second is listening. For developing wisdom peace of mind is imperative. You should try to attain the level of peace in your mind so that you can even listen to trees talking to you, sound of sunrays, sound of unborn child, sound of people's brain waves, and sound of others' heart beats.

Direction also dwells on a continuum from externally driven direction to strong inner direction. This comes from your personal mission, roles and goals of your life. It provides you the meaning to life and eliminates emptiness of life. Do not do things just because other people think it is a good idea. Go after your dreams, let them lead you. Give yourself permission to dream, go after that, let it lead you; it is the chance you have to move towards profound happiness (Covey 1989). Former Indian President Dr. A.P.J. Abdul Kalam in one of his deliberations to Indian students suggests to dreaming big with open eyes. One spiritual thought says that you cannot dream or imagine about what does not exist in this universe.

Choosing direction in life is not that important, it is more about fulfilment of your life with meaning, enthusiasm, and enjoyment. Offer something original to the world. Originality is always more important than quality, but the combination of both may provide a person prodigious results. People will respect you more for thinking and doing what they did not think of. Never lose the sight for the things that are fundamentally important to you and use them as landmarks to keep yourself on track.

The direction of our life may not be the same at every moment, rather it changes with time. It is important for us to always be ready to change our direction. It is not advisable to stay in a wrong situation for long and looking back on years and realizing that things could have been different. Be ready to revere your decisions. Remember course of life can be understood by looking backward but it must be lived by looking forward.

The **power** to take **action** should come from your own strengths and wisdom. Those who are dependent on others' emotions to take action become immobilize, and those who concentrate on their internal locus of control to generate power to take action turn into proactive persons and lead people successfully. You cannot win if you do not begin.

> *"My actions are my only true belonging. I cannot escape the consequences of my actions. My actions are the ground on which I stand."*
>
> Buddhist Sayings

Increase your knowledge by integrating and contemplating your vision and mission, experiences, and information you collect from the environment. Always carry a sense of responsibility for your destiny and problems. Develop ownership with them and raise the control over your actions. You can generate power to take action by developing a habit of finding and focusing on the wins of others, by keeping record of your own wins. Do not allow the imagination of losses and failures to guide your action. Try to assess the future consequences, but concentrate more on wins.

Assess your strengths, challenges, successes, values, roles and temperament. Take control of your thoughts, emotions and destiny. Discard self-defeating belief and attitudes. Learn to act not react. Learn to seek solutions not just face problems. Learn specific techniques to help you get unstuck and moving in the direction you have chosen for yourself.

In reality most of us are guided by external environment and unknowingly we keep others like family, spouse, friends, enemy, possessions, money, and pleasure, etc. at our centre, and with the result we are guided by others' strengths and weaknesses, and grow to be vulnerable to situations. In this case, we no longer generate our own strengths, wisdom, direction, and power to take action, instead it all comes from the person or things present at our centre and we make ourselves emotionally dependent on others. Normally, our centredness is changing from time to time and we keep one or two or combination of above-mentioned entities at our centre.

13

Personal Paradigm

In Section I, we have discussed various leadership concepts and could understand clearly that how leadership is different than managerial controls. It generates very good feeling while reading leadership concepts and we feel that we could easily apply these concepts in the real work setting and become good leaders. But in reality 90 per cent of our corporate managers are still struggling to become good leaders and not getting success in their leadership endeavours. The most difficult thing in the world is to become good leader though as mentioned earlier in this book that leadership can be learnt through passionate efforts.

In this regard, we have asked more than a hundred Indian corporate managers about their views on effectiveness of leadership concepts in the actual work settings. A majority of our respondents were in favour of managerial controls over leadership concept's application. According to them the participative leadership is the most difficult thing to implement at the workplace as most of the people have their own perceptions, personal biases against each other, personal greed to go high as early as possible, and possess serious disagreement with each other's approaches. Whenever they are entrusted with responsibility and empowered to do the job without any managerial controls they try to take advantage of no controls and showed non-compliance with their job routines. On the other hand, whenever these managers delegate the work autocratically with strong voice for compliance and put control systems to check everyone's work schedule and regular accomplishments, people showed better compliance and satisfactory performances.

Then we asked following questions to them:

- Whether people in your unit are generating the level of competence in the process that cannot be imitated by your competitors.
- Can you rate their performances as world-class performances?
- Are they generating excellence in the way of doing their work and doing it meticulously? Or simply doing it for the sake of doing?
- What is the level of their satisfaction with the company?
- Are they not willing to leave the company if the better opportunity is given to them?

The major percentage of honest answers to all the questions was BIG NO.

Now, you can understand the importance of leadership approaches and importance of commitment over compliance. In short-run managerial controls look very effective, but in the long-run it leads to poor performances and dissatisfaction among people.

There is no short cut for leaders. You need to do lots of ground work for successful implementation of leadership approaches. First of all you need to develop yourself as an integrated human being to work as role model to your followers and to nurture them to learn what to expect, how to perform the job excellently. For the above purposes you have to work on the development of your personal paradigm. You must acquire a certain level of physical, mental, and emotional acumen to win the trust of your followers, to develop mutual trust among people of the organization, and to develop synergy in the environment.

This section of the book is very essential for you to learn how to become integrated human being in order to utilize leadership concepts at the workplace and achieve real success.

> *"The process of becoming a leader is much the same as becoming an integrated human being."*
>
> Warren Bennis (1985)

Our personal paradigm whether it is correct or incorrect is the source of our attitude, behaviour, and ultimately our relationship with others. If we want to make minor changes in our life, we can perhaps appropriately focus on our attitude and behaviour, but if we want to make major change and want to become successful world-class leader, we need to work sincerely on our basic paradigm with the help of behavioural engineering. Behavioural engineering helps us to restructure our thought process, attitude, self-esteem, and behaviour. Our personal paradigm reflects our character that is the foundation in developing ourselves as a world-class leader.

Nowadays it is widely accepted fact that all humans are comprised of body, mind and emotions, so our real presence is based on our ability to manage three kinds of acumens: physical, mental and emotional. Yet we continue to overemphasize the development of our mental abilities. This over reliance on analytical abilities shuts us off from instinct, intuition, and creativity. A world-class leader as an integrated human being has a perfect blend of physical, mental and emotional acumen in his personal paradigm (Figure 13.1).

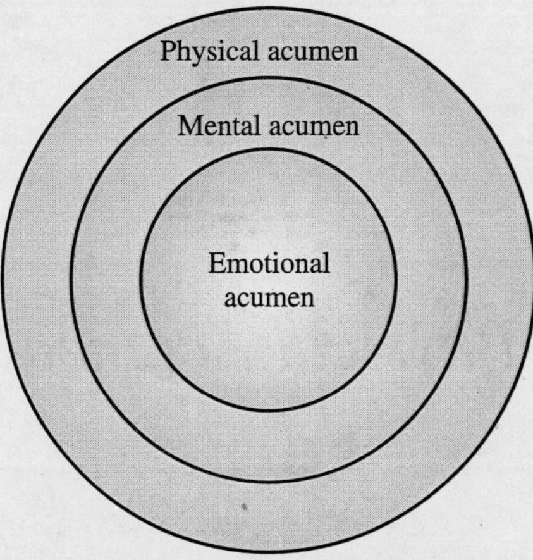

Figure 13.1 Personal paradigm.

14

Physical Acumen

People with physical acumen are grounded and present in their bodies. Know and respect the capacity and limits of their bodies. They are quite close to nature and rely on their physical "knowing" to respond intelligently to the world around them. They have good command on their language and are very effective in communications. Their body language is impressive and they have good dressing sense. Physically attuned persons know the following:

- What food is best for them.
- When they need rest.
- Physical boundaries of others and know how much space should be given to others.
- How to keep a body physically fit through yoga, exercise, and disciplined food intake.
- How well to get dressed so that they can make their presence felt.
- How to communicate empathically.
- How to develop precision in their speech and writings.

APPEARANCE AND ARTIFACTS

Potential employers, customers and colleagues are usually impressed by people who are trim, muscular and good in shape. People who look attractive are considered to be likable and persuasive, and they have generally successful careers. They also found to be credible more often than less attractive people.

Personal appearance is a major factor used to judge a person simply because the first impression of a person is based on appearance.

It is difficult to change your physical characteristics unless you go for plastic surgery to change the shape of your nose, lips, ear, etc. However, you can change your appearance by changing your clothing styles, hairstyles, and other accessories or artifacts such as glasses, jewellery, handkerchief, flowers and so on.

You may be surprised to know that some aspiring professionals may even turn for help to image consultants because appearance is such powerful force in business, you must always keep the following in mind:

- Pay attention to good grooming including a neat hairstyle, body hygiene, polished shoes and clear nails.
- Invest in professional looking clothing and accessories.
- Avoid flashy garments, chunky jewellery, garish make-up and overpowering perfumes.
- Ensure that you feel comfortable in your attire.

COMMUNICATION

As mentioned earlier the communication also reflects your physical acumen and is extremely useful in influencing as well as understanding others. Most of us allocate very little time to improve our communication, whereas it is one of the most important skills of a leader to enhance the productivity at the workplace. Following are some important benefits that effective communication can provide in the organization:

- It enhances your professional image.
- Helps you to build healthier business relationships.
- It improves customer relations.
- It helps you to align your employees with organization's vision and mission as well as to mentor them.
- Number of misunderstandings can be mitigated with effective communication.
- Better quality documents can be produced through good writing skills.
- Thoughts can be expressed in effective and precise manner.

Professor Albert Mehrabian (1971) established the following statistics which have now become a classic for the effectiveness of spoken communication:

- 7% of meaning is in the words that are spoken.
- 38% of meaning is paralinguistic (the manner in which the words are said).
- 55% of meaning is conveyed through facial expression.

SPOKEN COMMUNICATION TOOL KIT

As a speaker, there are several elements of oral communication of which you need to be aware in order to learn how to use them to your advantage. Let us begin with few rudimentary skills for interacting with the audience.

Eye Contact

Maintaining eye contact with your audience is the simplest thing you can do to establish a relationship. Eye contact serves many purposes. First, it establishes that the parties are listening. Second eye contact indicates respect. If a person is not making eye contact, they are less receptive to what you are about to say. Third eye contact is a basic expressive form. A speaker can learn a lot from the audience by just reading what their eyes are saying.

Body Language

As a speaker, the messages you send through your body language affect how your audience perceives you. Whether you are interacting one to one or with an auditorium of 200 people, the effectiveness of your message is affected by how you carry yourself. For example, when speaking to a large audience, crossing your arms is seen as bad body language. It shows that you as the speaker are closed off from the audience, which reflects negatively on your attitude towards the audience and your topic. You want your body language to establish interest and sincerity towards your audience.

Style and Register

Your tone and pace of speech affects how your audience responds to you. You want to match your tone to that of your audience. You do not want to come off as arrogant and ignorant. Rather, you need to sound confident at a basic level so that you do not lose credibility with your audience. The pace of your speech is also important. You can speak faster than you write and understand. You need to give your audience time to take in what you have just said, or you risk losing your audience. Try to stretch the gap within the words you pronounce in order to make it clearer. Develop attractive pronunciation by making conscious efforts everyday until it goes to your unconscious competence.

Paralanguage/Vocalic

You might have heard two of your colleagues talking to each other in a different language other than yours, though you could not understand the contents, you would have had some idea about their talk or at least their feelings, excitement, delight, frustration, exhaustion, or boredom from the tone of their voice and other non-verbal means. Voice communicates something beyond language. Paralanguage refers to all vocally produced sound that is not a direct form of linguistic communication.

This non-lexical vocal communication may be considered a type of non-verbal communication. This category includes number of sub-categories:

Tone

Tone is used to convey attitude. These may be direct, commanding, loud, harsh, disguised, soft, gentle, pleasing, sharp, rage and nasal, etc.

Voice inflection

The way we change the tone of our voice to emphasize key words. **Stressing** – I have got a BIG project. **Stretching**—I have got a b——i——g project. **Pausing**—I have got —————— a big project.

Pitch

Higher pitch—faster rate of vibration. Lower pitch—slower rate of vibration. Monotonous pitch throughout a conversation will be perceived as neither competent nor dynamic.

Intensity/Volume

Refer to loudness or softness of your voice. Weak voice—perceived as lack of confidence. Strong voice—shows great confidence.

Articulation

This is the process by which sounds syllables and words are formed when your tongue, jaw, teeth, lips, and palate alter the air stream coming from the vocal folds. Poor articulation often a result of years of bad habit. Attractive articulation can influence people to a great extent.

Quality

No two persons in the world have exactly the same voice. You can improve your quality of voice by perfect pitching with right modulation and suited volume in your voice.

Dysfluency

A dysfluency is any break in fluent speech. To generate the fluency in your spoken communication you need to first keep your deliberation at slower pace.

Tips for Effective Use of Non-verbal Communication

Some tips for the effective use of non-verbal communication are as follows:

- Observe and understand the non-verbal signals being sent your way on a moment–to–moment basis.
- Use good eye contact.
- Stop what you were doing when your listeners look glassy-eyed.
- Use the tone of your voice the way a musician uses an instrument. When you are expressing love, you can speak in soft lilting tones. When you are setting limits on a subordinate's behaviour you can use a tone of authority and firmness.
- Adopt the most appropriate posture that suits the occasion.
- Express gratitude to your audience when they are being attentive and responsive, the encouragement could increase the level of attentiveness and responsiveness, making it more enjoyable experience for you and for them.
- Soak in the pats/hugs that others give you. Many people have difficulty being present in the moment to truly receive the attention that comes with a hug or a pat. You need to stop resisting and try to express your happiness over that non-verbal signal.
- When you are confronting someone whom you are in close relationship with, reach out to take his/her hand in both of yours. This kind of gesture during a confrontation can assist the other person in hearing you instead of defending themselves.
- Understand the cultural nuances of the various forms of non-verbal communication.
- When there is a contradiction between the verbal and non-verbal messages of a person you are listening to, try to assess the situation with the help of non-verbal cues.

TIPS TO DEVELOP PHYSICAL ACUMEN

Though there is no one right way to develop your physical acumen, but we are trying to suggest some routines and practices to develop the same. A disciplined effort is needed to bring right routines and practices into your habits. A partial list of practices and routines is given below:

- Exercise everyday; this can include walking which is recommended over all other forms of activity.
- Take frequent time-out to breathe slowly and deeply.
- Get sufficient sleep; quality sleep is more important than the quantity.

- Avoid or moderate the eating of white sugar, white flour, salt, processed foods such as those found in cans, and factory-farmed meat, replacing with fresh foods whenever possible.
- Take high quality nutritional supplement everyday.
- Drink enough water.
- Give an hour everyday to polish your language; this you can do by speaking in isolation, simulating audience in front of you. While speaking, pronounce every word properly and stretch the gap within the words adequately.
- Concentrate on proper fitting and colour combination of your clothes according to occasion and time.
- Develop your positive body language and facial expressions (smile).
- Learn to keep eye contact while conversing with others.
- Keep adequate physical distance while interacting with others.
- Utilize your hand movement to support your oral communication.
- Learn to maintain correct body posture in different situations.

15

Mental Acumen

The mind is a powerful tool; keeping it healthy and active is vital for making sound business decisions, generating innovative solutions and to face environmental challenges. Leaders with good mental acumen have following qualities:

- Are expert in drill-down problem solving approach.
- Possess good conceptual and technical skills.
- Carry better quantitative aptitude.
- Have good reasoning ability.
- Have sharp memory and analytical power.

To improve mental acumen, there requires consistent efforts. One needs to allocate at least one hour everyday for this purpose. Following are some ways to improve your mental acumen:

Start using your weak hand

By switching the side of your mouse-pad you will force yourself to use your non-dominant hand. This, in turn, will stimulate the neural connections between the right and left hemispheres on your brain. Scientific research confirmed that people that use both hands equally have 10 per cent more nerve fibres joining the two sides of the brain. Ideally you want to perform as many activities as possible with your non-dominant hand, but some of them might become cumbersome. Using the mouse with the opposite hand or brushing your teeth with weak hand is something that you can easily integrate into your life. During the first couple of weeks it will feel unusual, and you might need to switch back when using programs that require intense "clicking" sessions. After this adaptation phase, however, you will be navigating the computer just as efficiently with both hands. Some musical instrument players who play their instruments with right hand have reported that when they played the same notation with their left hand for some time, they found that their right hand is moving more smoothly than before.

Force yourself to remember things

Sometimes you want to remember the name of a song that is playing or the name of an old acquaintance that passed by. It is right there, on the tip of your tongue, but you cannot remember it. What would you normally do in such situation? Probably ask some nearby friend for the name, and upon the disclosure you will even shout wondered, "Oh yeah! That is it." The next time this happens force yourself to remember that name. The brain can be stimulated just like your muscles and the more you exercise it the stronger it will get. Do not limit yourself to remembering names. Are you calling your mother to get the phone number of your uncle? Forget pen and paper, you can memorize it. Try to look at the keyboard of your phone in order to create a mental picture of what the sequence of numbers looks like.

Play games that involve some thinking

Games such as sudoku, crosswords, chess, scrabble, will already have a tangible impact upon your brain performance. Regularity is very important here, so try to incorporate these games or exercises into your routine. You could bring a crosswords book with you on the daily commute, for instance. Games like badminton, cricket, and tennis, etc. involve hand-eye coordination that stimulates the brain.

Take deep breath

More air in means more oxygen in the blood and therefore, in the brain. Breath through your nose and you will notice that you use your diaphragm more, drawing air deeper into your lungs. Several deep breaths can also help to relax you, which is conducive to clearer thinking.

Meditation

A simple meditation you can do right now is just closing your eyes and paying attention to your breath. Tensing up your muscles and then relaxing them to start may help. When your mind wanders, just bring your attention back to your breath. Five or ten minutes of this will usually relax you, clear your mind, and leave you more ready for any mental task.

Sit with straight posture

Posture affects your thinking process. Prove it to yourself by doing math in your head while slumping, looking at the floor and letting your mouth hang open. Then do the mental math while sitting up straight, keeping your mouth closed and looking forward or slightly upwards. You will notice that it is easier to think with the latter posture.

Good thinking habits

Just use a problem solving technique for several weeks and it will become a habit. Redesign everything you see for a while, and that will become a habit. You can develop many good thinking habits with some effort, and then be more resourceful effortlessly from that point on. Use the power of habit.

Use slack time

This is the time that is otherwise wasted or just under-utilized. Driving time, time spent in waiting rooms, or even time spent cleaning your room can be included in this. With a cassette player or CD player you can start to use this time to listen to books-on-tape or CD. You may spend 200 hours a year in your car or in waiting room. What could you learn in that time?

Learn a language

Learning a new language has been shown to halt the age-related decline in brain function. It also introduces your mind to new concepts and new ways of looking at things (in Hindi we are afraid, whereas in English we have fear). It is one of the best brain exercises.

Write

Writing is good for your mind in a number of ways. It is a way to tell your memory what is important, so you will recall things more easily in the future. It is a way to clarify your thinking. It is a way to exercise your creativity and analytical ability. Diaries, idea-journals, poetry, note-taking and story-writing are all ways to use writing to boost your brain power. Make a personal diary and start writing about your experiences and observations, everyday. It will certainly enhance your expression power, writing skills, skills for structuring the contents and finally your physical (communication) and mental acumen.

Sleep well

As long as you get a certain amount of sleep, probably a minimum of six hours, the quality seems to be more important than the quantity. Also, short naps in the afternoon seem to work well to recharge the brain for some people.

Avoid white sugar

Any simple carbohydrates can give you "brain fog." Sometimes called the "sugar blues" as well, this sluggish feeling makes it hard to think clearly. It results from the insulin rushing into the bloodstream to counteract the sugar rush. Avoid oily food, sugars, white bread and potato chips before any important mental tasks.

Read with fast pace

Contrary to what many believe, your comprehension of material often goes up when you learn to speed-read. You get to learn a lot more in less time, and it is definitely a good brain exercise.

Exercise

Long-term exercise can boost brainpower, which is not surprising. Anything that affects physical health in a positive way probably helps the brain too. Recent research, though, shows that cognitive function is improved immediately after just ten minutes of aerobic exercise. If you need a brain recharge, you might want to walk up and down the stairs a few times.

Imaginary person

Talking to and getting advice from characters in your mind can be a great way to access the information in your subconscious mind. Imagine a conversation with a person who has a lot of knowledge in the area you want advice in.

Do something you enjoy

This is a way to both lower stress and rev up your brain. The key is to do something active. Watching TV does not count. Whether it is playing scrabble or painting your house, when you are actively engaged in an activity that you enjoy, you worry less about things and you start to think better.

Walk

Exercise has been shown to benefit the brain, and walking is one of the best exercises for many. It is low impact, and the rhythmic nature of it seems to put you in a state that is very conducive to clear thinking. In fact, carry a tape recorder with you to take notes, and a twenty minute walk can be a great way to solve problems.

Model others

Find others that are creative, intelligent, or very productive. Do what they do, and think what they think. This is a key principle of neuro-linguistic programming. Be careful about taking their advice, though. Successful people often do not really understand why they are successful. Do what they do, not what they say.

Avoid unnecessary arguments

When you defend a position too vigorously, especially when it is just to "win" the argument, you invest your ego into it. This is not conducive to the easy acceptance and use of new information. In other words, you put your mind in a pothole, and you dig it deeper with each argument. Debate can be a valuable thing, but when the ego takes over, the mind closes a little. This is not a recipe for better thinking.

Laugh

The release of endorphins caused by laughter lowers stress levels, which is good for long-term brain health. Laughter also tends to leave you more open to new ideas and thoughts.

Self-awareness

This may not seem important to brain power, but it is. When you know yourself better, you can avoid the usual effects of ego and emotion in your seemingly "rational" thinking. Or you can at least take it into account. Watch yourself, especially as you explain things or argue.

Eat less and increase antioxidants in your diet

Overeating has the immediate effect of redirecting more blood to the digestive process, leaving less for the brain. Long-term, it can cause arterial obstructions that reduce blood flow to the brain permanently. In at least one study, rats on a restricted-calorie diet had more brainpower. Take food that has quite a good amount of antioxidants, e.g. spinach.

Develop your intuition

Intuition is often referred to as "gut instinct," that physical sense we get when we know if a choice is right or wrong, or if a person is trustworthy or not. Intuition can be an important part of brainpower. Einstein and others have relied heavily on their intuitive hunches. Figure 15.1 is the model to develop intuitive skills. To develop intuitive skills you need to be involved regularly in observing things happening around with open mind followed by listening and reading. The first step in developing and refining your intuitive skills is learning the art of observation. You should also be involved in taking actions means doing things and learn from experience gained in the process. One of the keys to establishing power and control over your life is to spend part of each day alone and to use that time to reflect your current feelings and challenges. Making time for contemplation leads to new realizations and important discoveries that can easily slip through the cracks of our busyness. The contemplation on information and experience gathered through above mentioned techniques will develop your intuitive skills to the maximum. Therefore, contemplation is extremely important to develop intuitive skills. Anything that takes us out of the body and out of our self-awareness takes us farther away from our instincts and intuition. For real contemplation you should also look within, look around and look beyond the horizons. If you watch recent trends and future trends, you can have intuitive skills. Those with better intuitive skills can unfold the future in present and effectively visualize that what would be the scenario after five years. Developing such practice is additionally important because we receive information through our subconscious minds through one of the way. In our hyperactive, fast-paced lives, we prevent ourselves from tapping into the subconscious stream, which contains knowledge, and impressions that might be very valuable, for example a fine connection between two seemingly unrelated events that sheds new light on a situation.

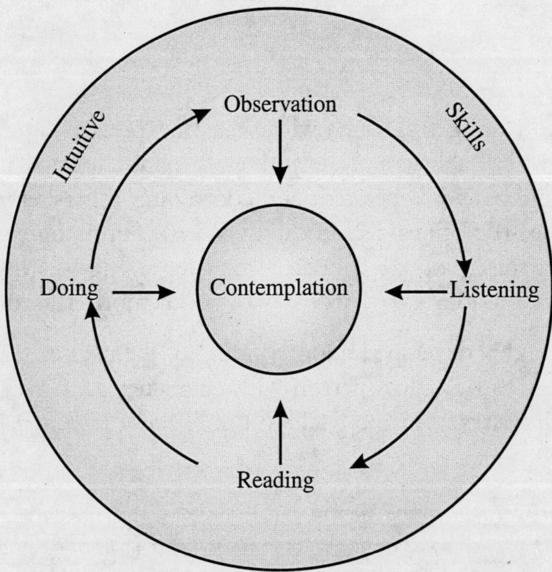

Figure 15.1 Model to develop intuitive skills.

16

Emotional Acumen

The more you can get in touch with your unexpressed emotions, the more easily you will be able to activate your emotional acumen. This will lead you to become emotionally independent and controlling others' emotions through gaining expertise in emotional reciprocation. When your thoughts, emotions, and actions are consistent, you are connected to your strengths, wisdom, direction and power to take actions. Most people with good emotional acumen:

- Have a highly developed understanding of themselves, and use that self-awareness to become a person with character. As Covey (1989) wrote about character in his best selling book, *Seven Habits of Highly Effective People:*

  "If somebody tries to use human influence strategies and tactics of how to get other people to do what he wants, to work better, to be liked by others, and mean while his character is flawed, marked by duplicity and insincerity, in the long-run he cannot be successful. His duplicity will breed distrust and everything he does – even using the so-called good human relation techniques will be perceived as manipulative. There are people we trust absolutely because we know their character. Whether they are eloquent or not, whether they have human relation techniques or not, we trust them, and we work successfully with them".

- Are aware of their thoughts, moods, and feelings.
- Have strong self-control over their emotional impulses and are aware of the effects of noxious emotions.
- Have highly developed social skills and are able to harmonize with others.

Emotional acumen allows a person to control his or her emotions that he or she is experiencing and develops synergy in the environment. By changing the way, we think we change the emotions we are experiencing.

To develop your emotional acumen, you need to concentrate on two basic models of emotional acumen that are emotional autonomy and emotional reciprocation. The emotional autonomy model deals with person's self-control, self-awareness, and emotional independency. The emotional reciprocation model helps individuals to develop productive relationship with people.

EMOTIONAL AUTONOMY

Many research observations have indicated that successful leaders have certain personality traits. They are always guided by their own set of rules and values and do not get affected by external forces. The emotional autonomy model works on various dimensions that make them emotionally independent. Those dimensions are given in the emotional autonomy model given in Figure 16.1.

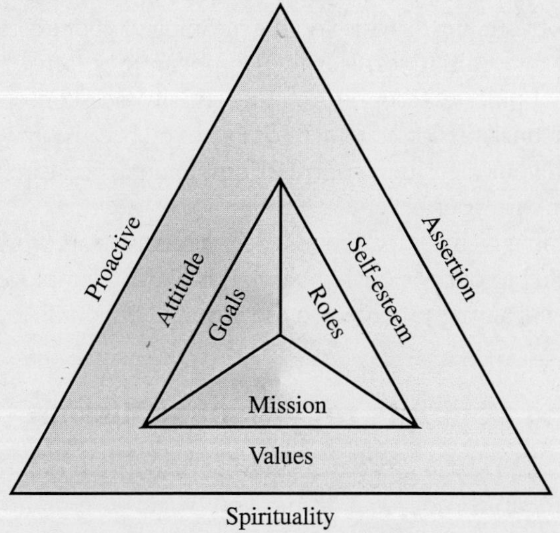

Figure 16.1 Dimensions of emotional autonomy.

MISSION

A **personal mission statement** is a brief description of what you want to focus on, what you want to accomplish and who you want to become in a particular area of your life over the next one to three years. It is a way to focus your energy, actions, behaviours and decisions towards the things that are most important to you. It is an important tool that provides you emotional anchorage so that you can be firm, stable and focused in adverse situations.

A personal mission statement based on correct principles become the same kind of standard for an individual as the constitution for the country (Covey 1989). Personal mission provides purpose to life that brings passion. Mission fills the emptiness of life with full of meaning. Purpose of life resolves the conflict between self interest and social obligations.

> *"If the universe is an accident, we are accident. But if there is meaning in the universe there is meaning is us also."*
>
> Albert Einstein

The high achievers even if they are working as professionals in large corporation view themselves as self-employed. They have a sense of personal mission and take proactive approach to create results what they want to. They are always guided by their mission statement and take full responsibility for fulfilling their mission regardless of external conditions. In contrast, average people view themselves as employees and always guided by ups and downs in the environment. If you want to be in the top 3 per cent of achievers' group, you must make your personal mission as your employer. The personal mission is a kind of employer that fulfils the emptiness of your life, provide you the meaning of your existence, inspiration, motivation to take initiatives, learning opportunities, sense of achievement, satisfaction, happiness, recognition, and finally self-concept. Writing and reviewing a personal mission statement changes you because it forces you to think deeply through your priorities, contributions, and passion carefully and to align your behaviour with your beliefs.

No matter in which company and under whom you are working, your actual employer should be your personal mission. It is a kind of employer who will never ditch you and will always provide you the meaning of your life.

How to Find Contents for Personal Mission

According to Frankl (1984), "we detect rather than invent our mission of life". A mission statement is not something you write overnight. It takes deep introspection, careful analysis, thoughtful expression and often many rewrites to produce it in final form. It may take several weeks or even months before you feel really comfortable with it. You must incorporate your values and directions in your personal mission. You may follow the following steps to develop personal mission statement:

Write down your past successes

Identify your four to five moments when you have had personal success at your workplace, community, or at home in recent years. Review your accomplishments.

List of core values

Develop a list of your core values with which you identify yourself as what kind of person you are.

Think about your future contribution

Identify and list down your strengths. Based on your strengths, make a list of the ways through which you can make the difference. Mention how you can contribute best to this world in general, your family, employer, friends, and community, etc.

List your priorities, and interests

Spend some time thinking about your priorities in life and your personal goals. Also explore the areas in which you have keen interests and passion to get involved.

Write mission statement

Integrate and contemplate on above prepared lists, and start writing your personal mission statement.

Guidelines to Write Personal Mission Statement

Following points should be kept in mind while writing the personal mission statement:

- Keep it simple, clear and brief. The best mission statements tend to be 3 to 5 sentences long.
- Your mission statement should touch upon what you want to focus on and who you want to become as a person (character) in this part of your life. Think about specific actions, behaviours, habits and qualities that would have a significant positive impact in this part of your life over the next one to three years.
- Make sure your mission statement is positive. Instead of saying what you do not want to do or do not want to be, say what you do want to do or become. Find the positive alternatives to any negative statements.
- Include positive behaviours, character traits and values that you consider particularly important and want to develop further.
- Think about how your actions, habits, behaviour and character traits in this area affect the important relationships in your life.
- Create a mission statement that will guide you in your day-to-day actions and decisions. Make it a part of your everyday life.
- Think about how your mission affects the other areas of your life.
- Make it emotional and along with emotions infuse it with your passion. That will make it even more compelling, inspiring and energizing.

Example of Personal Mission Statement

"I want to learn various ways to become integrated human being, provide knowledge to Indian youth to transform them into world-class leaders who can bring peace and harmony in the society, develop quality standards and competences in their organizations. I believe in my role, not in the position. I consider myself as right person, not a nice person. I work with intent to contribute, not to control".

ROLES AND GOALS

Each of us have a number of different roles in our lives, different areas or capacities in which we have responsibility. You may, for example, have a role as an individual, husband or wife, father or mother, teacher, manager, scientist, consultant, and so on. You may find that your mission statement will be much more balanced, much easier to work with, if you break it down into the specific role areas of your life and the goals you want to accomplish in each area.

Roles and goals give structure and organized direction to your personal mission. An effective goal focuses primarily on results rather than activity. It identifies where you want to be and in the process, helps you determine where you are. Set your long-term and short-term goals for each role. To create change in your life, you need to focus on what you want, not on what you do not want. If you keep focusing on what you do not want, you will just get more of the same. While setting your goals always see the objectives not the obstacles.

Goals can help you to become more decisive and directed on a daily basis. They will help you focus your energies in a positive way to achieve the life you desire. Goals provide motivation to make an effort to achieve success in life. Think about football game without goal post, neither you will get any excitement of watching the game, nor players would have any motivation to move forward.

Goals are dreams with deadline and an action plan. Support your goals by direction, dedication, determination, discipline and deadlines. Your personal goals must be specific and realistic, measurable, attainable, rewarding and bounded with timelines.

To achieve your goals, you need to develop strategy of action plans. The goals are actually the end-results that you want to accomplish and the action plans are the means to achieve desired end-results. Goals require persistence, and means to achieve them required flexibility. If you face difficulties and unexpected problems use all your persistence and determination to stick to your goals, but always stay flexible with your strategies or action plans. If one way is not working try another until you find one that works. Do not change the ends, change the means, and never forget the difference between ends and means.

Guidelines to Set Personal Goals

Our goal may be challenging or far-reaching but it should not be out of sight. Following are some points you must consider while setting your personal goals:

- Be specific about your goals and define them in as much detail as possible. For example, if your goal is to buy a new car, write down a specific model. Get a picture of the car you want and visualize yourself driving it.
- Your personal goals should be believable, yet challenging. By setting challenging goals, you must keep yourself outside the comfort zone and enable yourself to grow and do progress in life. Your personal goals must be aligned with your basic values. This means that you must set goals that are consistent with what you believe to be good, right and important.
- The best way to start is to write down everything you would like to accomplish on a piece of paper. Divide the list into different heads according to your roles. Writing down your goals will support you in manifesting what you want more readily. Review them often; even 15 minutes a day will keep you committed to create your new life. If you really want to make things happen for you start writing something down.
- All goals should be written in present positive tense, as if you had already achieved that goal. They should also be specific and with as much details as possible.
- They should also include a date or deadlines and if appropriate should be measurable. This will allow you to monitor your progress.

ATTITUDE

Attitude is how you see persons, things or any situation, negatively or positively? The adversity or desirability of a situation is not that important for our success or failure, but our attitude towards it is what really matters. You can make progressive changes in your life and make things happen for you by just modifying your attitudes of mind. In the corporate world, 85 per cent success in getting jobs and promotions are because of attitude and only 15 per cent because of intelligence and knowledge of facts and figures. Your goal, your desire, is to be as successful, happy and prosperous as you possibly can be in every aspect of your life. Therefore, the systematic and purposeful development of a positive mental attitude is something that you need to work in every hour. If your attitude is negative, your life is restricted. You cannot pretend to smile for a long unless you have the desire to serve. When smile is not sincere it is irritating.

Various Ways to Assure Positive Attitude

There are various things you can do to assure that your attitude is the very best it can be under all circumstances.

Keep your focus on future

Whatever challenges you face, focus on the future rather than on the past. Instead of worrying about who did what and who is to blame, focus on where you want to be and what you want to do. Get a clear mental image of your ideal successful future, and then take whatever action you can to begin moving in that direction. Let the past take care of itself, and get your mind, your thoughts, and your mental images on the future.

Be a part of the solution

Whenever you are faced with a difficulty, focus on the solution rather than on the problem. Think and talk about the ideal solution to the obstacle or setback, rather than wasting time rehashing and reflecting on the problem. Solutions are inherently positive, whereas problems are inherently negative. The instant that you begin thinking in terms of solutions, you become a positive and constructive human being.

Try to search positive aspects in all situations

Assume that something good is hidden within each difficulty or challenge. Dr. Norman Vincent Peale, a major proponent of positive thinking, once said, "Whenever God wants to give us a gift, he wraps it up in a bundle of problems." There is always positive in a person or a situation, but you have to dig deep and remove lots of dirt (negative) to look for positive. For instance, a miner removes tones of dirt to find gold or diamond. So change your focus and look for positive. Count your blessings not your troubles.

Always seek learning opportunities

Assume that whatever situation you are facing at the moment is exactly the right situation you need to ultimately be successful. This situation has been sent to you to help you learn something, to help you become better, to help you expand and grow. In every challenge, look for the valuable lesson. Assume that every setback contains a lesson that is essential for you to learn. Only when you learn this lesson you will be smart enough and wise enough to go on to achieve the big goals that you have set for yourself.

Face criticism

Take criticism as blessings and opportunity to learn. Always think about your contribution and how you can add value. It takes character to listen to critics. Average people avoid criticism and guarantee that they remain average.

Believe in doing

Only positive attitude will not bring any success. Making an effort with positive attitude is important. Having positive attitude without making the effort is nothing more than having wishful dream. Make a habit of doing it now. Many persons are poor in making decision or taking action because they do lots of analysis and embrace paralysis by over analysis. Therefore, avoid paralysis by analysis and do not leave things for tomorrow that you can do today.

Learn from your mistakes

Do not rationalize your mistakes. Analyze and learn from them.

Persistence

Persistence is a decision. It is a commitment to finish what you start. When we are exhausted, quitting looks good but winners endure.

Give more than you get

There is no competition for extra mile, try to be more valuable and to see how you can add value. You will find that people have started seeing you as a leader and you are commanding respect from your senior.

Attitude has two important supporting components, they are discipline and invincible thinking.

Discipline

Discipline is an important ingredient of attitude that helps us to stay focused and take actions. It takes self-control, sacrifice, and avoiding distractions and temptations. Most of us have wrong understanding about discipline as we consider it as barrier to our freedom. But in reality discipline gives freedom. Freedom is not procured by full enjoyment of what is desired, but controlling the desire (*From The Golden Sayings of Epictetus*). Discipline is loving firmness. It is prevention before problem arises and allows us to go high in the adverse circumstances. You cannot live your life by emotions alone. You need to add discipline, no matter of what age you are. All the top personalities in various field reached on top because they have incorporated discipline along with their talents while making efforts.

To develop self discipline you need to come out of your comfort zone and stretch yourself to accomplish challenging tasks. You need to work on your four important pillars of self discipline that are:

- Acceptance of challenging tasks.
- Willpower to stretch yourself to come out of your comfort zone.
- Hard work diligently to accomplish the tasks.
- Persistence for sticking to tasks even in extremely adverse situations.

Many people waste their talent or failed to achieve the height in commensuration to their talent because of lack of discipline. The talent is raw material and to convert it into a meaningful product, disciplined efforts must be added to it. The disciplined efforts consists focus, time management (adequate allocation of time for each of the activities), regular polishing of talent with rigorous practice, and persistence.

Invincible Thinking

Another constituent of attitude is invincible thinking the term given by Okawa (2007). Invincible thinking will provide you the strength to find solution even for the toughest problem. It provides the dynamite to blast through solid rock, a drill to bore through all the barriers until you achieve your goals.

Life has good times and bad times. Invincible thinking will help you to provide the greatest nourishment to your soul at adverse situation. You can learn most important lesson in your bad times.

Albert Einstein observed that, "The significant problem we face cannot be solved at the same level of thinking we were at when we created them. We need a new level, a deeper level of thinking to solve a problem." This new level of thinking is invincible thinking. It suggests that there is a solution to every problem, you have to find it. Invincible thinking adopts inside-out approach means to start first with self, even more fundamentally to start with most inside part of self–with your paradigm.

It also advises that if you think you can or if you think you cannot, you are right. Invention is a vital element of invincible thinking. You need to identify a problem for the reason that all the problems are buried under thick layers of various symptoms. Once the problem is identified and the solution is not available within the present knowledge and experience, you need to move beyond your boundaries and have to invent the solution with the help of innovative ideas.

We basically face three categories of problems on which we have direct control, indirect control and no control. The direct control problem involves our own behaviour and it can be solved easily by exploring and changing our own behaviour. Indirect control problems involve other people's behaviour and there are number of solutions, but most of us have only three or four of those in our repertoire, and if that does not work we take either flight or fight. How liberating it is to accept the idea that I can learn new methods of human influence instead of constantly trying to use old ineffective methods to shape up someone else? Lastly with no control problems we can do nothing about, we need to accept and learn to live with them.

VALUES

Values, personal values, and core values all refer to the same thing. They are desirable qualities, standards, or principles. Values are a person's driving force and influence his/her actions and reactions. Some of the common values are bravery, generosity, acceptance, beauty, commitment, excellence, family, fun, harmony, health, leadership, love, prestige, respect, spirituality, wealth, service, sincerity, etc.

Value is a meaningful philosophy or a belief of all people that they embrace from their culture, religion, social system, family, schools, and/or organizations they are working for. All human beings possess a core set of values (ethical, business, or social values). They may or may not be aware of their core values, but they are always guided by their values or belief. Values can range from commonplace such as the belief in hard work and punctuality, to the more psychological such as self-reliance, concern for others, and harmony of purpose.

Values are psychological entities that generate enormous amount of psychological energy that always attract success, achievement and well-being. Though we cannot see or physically feel our values, but they are always present with us as factual as any physical entity. People may dedicate their entire lives or even give up their lives to pursue their values, as so many loyal patriots have fought for values of freedom, equality and human rights during the past two centuries.

We all have values that determine our decisions and guide our lives. Those who value their individuality, take responsibility, are self-reliant and act with self-respect. Those who value truthfulness, cannot bring themselves to tell a lie. Those who value family or friendship, sacrifice their personal interests for the good of others. Those who value goodness, cannot bring themselves to do something they know is wrong. We express values in our relations with other people when we are loyal, reliable, honest, generous, trusting, trustworthy, feel a sense of responsibility for family, friends, co-workers, our organization, community or country. On a more physical level, we may place great value on cleanliness, punctuality, orderliness, accuracy, quality, and physical perfection in whatever we do.

People who do not know their values or guided by negative belief tend to wander around, bouncing from one thing to another, trying to find themselves. They are like puppets, pulled along without any clear direction. Knowing your values helps you to:

- Follow a clear set of rules and guidelines for your actions. You are less likely to take the easy way out or chase after short-term gains at the expense of your long-term goals.
- Make good decisions. You quickly know what good choices are for you and what are not.
- Find compatible people, places, and things that support your way of living.
- Live with integrity. Integrity here does not mean honesty or honour. Integrity means wholeness or completeness, being a whole person. Nothing left out. Being true to yourself.

Values, Accomplishment, and Our Psychological Energies

Accomplishment in life depends not only on physical energy, but even more on the intensity of *psychological* energy, we are able to bring to our action. Interest, commitment, determination, passion, drive, enthusiasm are some of the ways in which we characterize the intensity of our psychological energy. It turns out that value directs our psychological energies for accomplishment. The gymnast or figure skater with a passion for perfection will continue to practice throughout her career to sharpen his/her skills, moved by the search for the value of perfection that score of perfect 10. Thus, we see that values determine the intensity and flow of our psychological energies.

Just as an individual the organizations as a whole are also guided by their values. The kind of guiding values of any particular organization and the commitment of all the employees with the same actually decides the amount of success for the organization. In fact, employees' commitment to organizational values generates ample psychological energy in the environment that produces excellent performances.

Core Values of a Leader

Harmony

Harmony is the coming together of disparate elements for common purpose. It is the moving together of varied or opposing forces, so that they emerge in a higher truth that all can benefit from (not merely a compromised truth). The value of Teamwork is one variation of the value of Harmony, as is the value of Organization. Harmony is such noble and elevated a value that it can be considered a *spiritual* value.

Make harmony a permanent personal value that you believe in and practice. Over the next few weeks notice points of conflict that appear in your work and life and seek to implement an action in each situation that can harmonize the opposing ideas, conflicts between people.

Concern for others

Perhaps the singlemost powerful way to succeed in life is to have more concern for our fellow human beings. Normally, we are overwhelmingly concerned about our own selves, driven by our own personal motives and ambitions. However, the happiest people literally lose themselves in the feelings, thoughts, and aspirations of others.

Are you ready to "forget yourself" and be genuinely interested in the welfare of others? Are you willing to be tolerant and kind to others, listen attentively and silently to their words, be non-judgmental, and open to their opinions and points of view? If you are able to do this, you are an excellent candidate to become world-class leader, not to mention an ever-increasing personal happiness and joy.

Try a little experiment. When you meet others, immediately put yourself in their shoes. Think only of what they want. Listen carefully to their thoughts and feelings, and show genuine concern and empathy. Do this for the entire meeting. Now, watch how the interaction goes. Watch how the energy level of the other person increases. The other individual becomes more animated and involved.

Commitment

Commitment says the following:

- I am willing to sacrifice because I care.
- I am a person of integrity and you can trust me.
- I will not let you down in good times or bad times.
- Despite pain I will still be there.

Honesty

Honesty means there are no contradictions or discrepancies in thoughts, words, and actions. It implies a refusal to lie. Honesty requires true expression of feelings towards others in interpersonal relationships. It also indicates your adherence with truth.

Individual dignity

One of the most significant personal value is to look on every person as an extraordinary, distinctive individual. This form of deep sense of respect for each person has the power of generating goodwill, immense happiness, and enormous achievement.

As a leader develop your personal system of values and translate your values in work life.

SELF-ESTEEM

> *No one can make you feel inferior without your permission.*
>
> Eleanor Roosevelt (1937)

Self-esteem is how we feel about ourselves. Our self-esteem develops and evolves throughout our lives as we build an image of ourselves through our experiences with different people and activities. Experiences during our childhood play a particularly large role in the shaping of our basic self-esteem. In the growing stage, our successes (and failures) and how we were treated by the members of our immediate family, teachers, coaches, and peers, all contributed to the creation of our basic self-esteem.

Our past experiences, even the things we do not usually think about, are all alive and active in our daily life in the form of an *internal voice*. Although most people do not "hear" this voice in the same way they would a spoken one, in many ways it acts in a similar way, constantly repeating those original messages to us. For people with healthy self-esteem, the messages of the inner voice are positive and reassuring. For people with low self-esteem, the internal voice becomes a ruthless inner critic, constantly criticizing, punishing, and ridiculing their accomplishments.

For people with good basic self-esteem, normal "ups and downs" may lead to temporary fluctuations in how they feel about themselves, but only to a limited extent. In contrast, for people with poor basic self-esteem, these "ups and downs" may make all the difference in the world.

People with high self-esteem grow in conviction, competence and willingness to accept responsibility. They compete against themselves and compare their performance with their capabilities. Whereas people with low self-esteem are close minded, pretend that they know everything, and justify their failures and compare their performance against others' achievements. Table 16.1 shows the differences between high and low self-esteem characteristics.

TABLE 16.1 High Self-Esteem vs Low Self-esteem

High Self-esteem	*Low Self-esteem*
Talk about ideas	Talk about people
Respects authority	Rebels against authority
Concerned about character	Concerned about reputation
Assertive behaviour	Aggressive behaviour
Willing to learn	Know it all
Solitude—Creative when they are alone	Lonely—Uncomfortable when alone
Discuss	Argue
Internally driven	Externally driven
Giver	Taker

Consequences of Low Self-esteem

Low self-esteem can have devastating consequences:

- It can create anxiety, stress, loneliness and increased likelihood for depression.
- It can cause problems with friendships and relationships.
- It can seriously impair academic and job performance.
- It can lead to underachievement and increased vulnerability to drug and alcohol abuse.
- It can make you involved in criminal activities.
- It can force you to gain sadistic pleasure.

Persons with low self-esteem possess only positional authority and do not command respect from their followers. They are poor listener and carry "know it all" attitude, do not understand the humour and become over sensitive against their criticism. Their behaviour is unpredictable and they start using positional authority over others to dictate their terms and generate sadistic pleasure.

Worst of all, these negative consequences themselves reinforce the negative self-image and can take a person into a downward spiral of lower and lower self-esteem and increasingly non-productive or even actively self-destructive behaviour. As a leader you must believe on your capabilities and should make sure that you see yourself capable and confident person.

Three steps to improve uour self-esteem

To become a world-class leader you need to have high self-esteem that you can improve by the three steps. Before you can begin to improve your self-esteem you must first believe that you can change it. Change does not necessarily happen quickly or easily, but it can happen. You are not powerless! Once you have accepted, or are at least willing to entertain the possibility that you are not powerless, the three steps you can take to begin to change your self-esteem are:

STEP 1: Invalidate the internal critic's voice

The first important step in improving self-esteem is to begin to challenge the negative messages of the critical internal voice. Here are some typical examples of the internal critic's voice and how you can invalidate that voice.

TABLE 16.2 Invalidation to Internal Critic's Voice

Internal Critic's Voice	*Your Invalidations*
It is ruthless: "The higher management liked my presentation, but it was not up to any standard. Actually people could not notice my mistakes. I am such a manipulator."	**Encourage yourself:** "Great, my presentation was highly appreciated by management. Maybe there were some mistakes, but I worked hard on that presentation and put my honest efforts. I am happy with myself. This was a fantastic endeavour."
Unrealistic generalization: "I could not achieve the targets. I am very poor worker and I do not have potential to survive in this company, better I should leave this company before I am thrown out by higher management."	**Analyze proactively:** "Yes I could not achieve the targets but I made my honest efforts. I am performing consistently since last three years. Let us look where I went wrong at this time and what are other factors that are responsible."
Jumping to irrational conclusion: "The face reaction of my colleague is erratic with me. He is annoyed with me. May be he does not like me any more.	**Be emotionally independent:** "The face reaction of my colleague is erratic with me, but I have not done any thing wrong against him. May be he has his personal problems. I will help him to solve his problem."

STEP 2: Practice self-nurturing

Invalidating your critical internal voice is an important first step, but it is not enough. Since our self-esteem is in part due to how others have treated us in the past, the second step to more healthy self-esteem is to begin to treat you as a worthwhile person.

Start to challenge past negative experiences or messages by nurturing and caring for yourself in ways that shows you are valuable, competent, deserving and lovable. There are several components to self-nurturing that are as hereunder:

Practice basic self-care

Get enough sleep, eat in a healthy fashion, get regular exercise, practice good hygiene, and so forth.

Plan fun and relaxing things for yourself

You could go to a movie, take a nap, get a massage, plant a garden, buy a pet, and learn to meditate—whatever you enjoy.

Reward yourself for your accomplishments

You could take the day off to celebrate good grades, spend time with a friend, or compliment yourself for making that hard work.

Remind yourself of your strengths and achievements

One way is to make a list of things you like about yourself. Or keep a *success* file of awards, certificates and positive letters or citations. Keep mementos of accomplishments you are proud of where you can see them.

Forgive yourself when you do not do all you hoped

Self-nurturing can be surprisingly hard if you are not used to doing it. Do not be critical of yourself remember that inner voice! when you do not do it just right.

Self-nurture even when you do not feel you deserve it

"Fake it" until you can "make it." When you treat yourself like you deserve to feel good and be nurtured, slowly you will come to believe it.

STEP 3: Get help from others

Getting help from others is often the most important step a person can take to improve his or her self-esteem, but it can also be the most difficult. People with low self-esteem often do not ask for help because they feel they do not deserve it. But since low self-esteem is often caused by how other people treated you in the past, you may need the help of other people in the present to challenge the critical messages that come from negative past experiences. Here are some ways to get help from others:

Ask for support from friends

- Ask friends to tell you what they like about you or think you do well.
- Ask someone who cares about you to just listen to your "vent" for a little while without trying to "fix" things.
- Ask for a hug.
- Ask someone who loves you to remind you that they do.

Get help from teachers and other helpers

- Go to professors or advisors or tutors to ask for help in classes if this is a problem for you. Remember that they are there to help you learn!
- If you lack self-confidence in certain areas, take classes or try out new activities to increase your sense of competence (for example, take a math class, join a dance club, take swimming lessons, etc.)

Talk to a therapist or counsellor

- Sometimes low self-esteem can feel so painful or difficult to overcome that the professional help of a therapist or counsellor is needed.
- Talking to a counsellor is a good way to learn more about your self-esteem issues and begin to improve your self-esteem.

PROACTIVITY

Proactivity is one of the most popular management buzzwords to come from the 1990s. Yet there are a number of definitions of what it means to be proactive.

In the Oxford dictionary, proactive means controlling your circumstances by making things happen.

Many would argue that being proactive means to take action on an issue before being asked. Stephen Covey has defined proactivity as more than merely taking the initiative, it is about understanding your responsibility to take the initiatives. Many organizations that are emphasizing on team based structures need proactive work culture so that people feel themselves responsible and accountable even for the work not allocated to them.

Frankl (1984) gave the proactive model based on stimulus response theory that describes that proactive persons have freedom to choose there responses based on their self awareness, imagination, conscience, and independent will, whereas reactive persons react to stimulus and give reactions according to stimulus. No one can snatch the power from you to choose you response in any given situation. In other words, no one can control your emotions and thoughts unless you allow doing so.

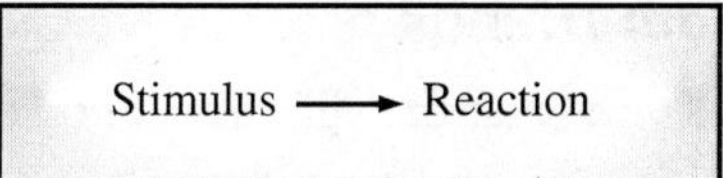

Figure 16.2 Reactive model.

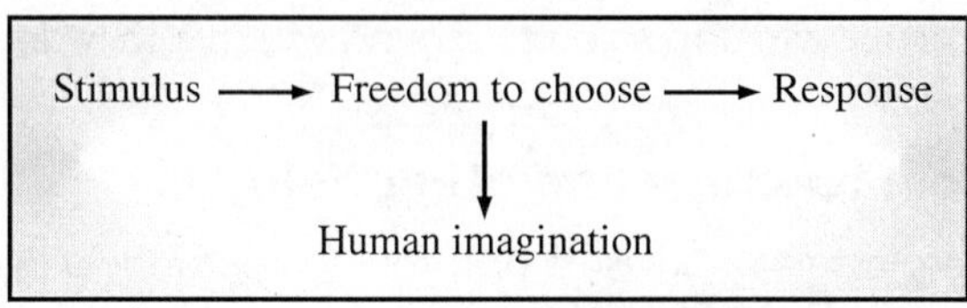

Figure 16.3 Proactive model: There is freedom to choose response.

Covey (1989) further elaborates that proactive persons possess responsibility, i.e., response + ability. This means proactive persons have ability to choose their responses in any situation. They are not controlled by their circumstances and they understand that they are responsible for their own life; they do not blame their circumstances, conditions or conditioning for their behaviour. Their behaviour is the product of their own conscious choice, based on values, rather than product of their conditions.

Reactive people are often affected by their physical environment. When people treat them well they feel well; when people do not they become defensive or protective. Reactive people build their lives around the behaviour of others, empowering the weaknesses of other people to control them. Researches are indicating that majority of people that belong to Indian culture possess external attribution and spend their whole life analyzing other's behaviour, traits, systems and environment. They do not give even 1 per cent of their time to explore themselves about their behaviour, personal mission, interests, skills, strengths, values and the level of self-esteem existing in them. Proactive persons always carry internal focus and regularly involved in exploring positives and negatives of their own behaviour, try to enhance their self-esteem, and always refer to their personal mission, roles, goals and values in any given situation.

Proactive Language

Our language is very real indicator of the degree to which we see ourselves as proactive people. The language of reactive people absolves them of responsibility. They say, "there is nothing I can do", "that is just the way I am", "he makes me so mad", and "he will not allow that", etc. Whereas the language of proactive people embraces responsibility, they say, "Let us look our alternatives", "I can choose a different approach", "I can control my own feelings", and "I can make an effective presentation".

Internal and External Focus

The concept of "internal and external focus" is generated from the theory of "internal locus of control" by Rotter in 1966. Locus of control refers to an individual's perception about the underlying main causes of events in his life. Individual believes that his behaviour is guided by his personal preference and efforts.

People with internal focus; concentrate into their inner paradigm on which they have full control, to adjust themselves with environment, whereas persons with external focus; concentrate on external environment to adjust themselves with environment. External environment contains people, situational realities, and circumstances on which we do not have control or have some indirect control.

Reactive people possess external focus. They are guided by the weaknesses of other people, the problems in the environment and circumstances. They empower things within external environment to control them. The negative energy generated by that focus, combined with neglect in areas where they could do something about, causes their inner paradigm and strengths to shrink.

Proactive people have internal focus. They work on their inner paradigm, on the things they can do something about. This generates the positive energy and enlarges their inner paradigm and strength to make decisions. They are not guided by others' weaknesses, and their behaviour and decisions are guided by their own preferences. The language in internal focus is filled with BEs. That is, I can be more patient, be wise, be more resourceful, be more diligent, and be more cooperative, etc. You cannot achieve marvelous things in life unless you start concentrating on your own efforts and believing that you have the potential, courage and confidence to control your circumstances.

ASSERTIVE BEHAVIOUR

The leadership behaviour may range from passive, assertive to aggressive behaviour.

Passive Behaviour

Passive behaviour tends to be associated with conflict avoidance, suppressing one's own needs, wanting the approval of others, and being inhibited and submissive. These traits are not considered effective for leadership. The passivity is based on unknown fear, fear of failure, fear for rejection, fear of retaliation, fear of hurting others and being hurt, and fear of getting into trouble, etc. Passive people try to accommodate others' wishes without standing for their own right. They often have very poor self-esteem and are unhappy.

Aggressive Behaviour

Aggressive behaviour is the opposite of passiveness. Aggressive people are self-centred, have little concern for the feelings or rights of others, and tend to be dominating and pushy. This behaviour seems effective for getting things done, but frequently creates resistance and resentment.

Aggressive people are demanding, rude and dominating. They want their own ways and force to gain control. For winning in any interpersonal conflict they will not hesitate to cheat to gain control. They always rationalize their action by saying "everything is fair in love and war". They have the tendency to violate the rights of others to get their way. They appear to be self-confident, but their behaviour is more often result of poor self-concept. Although they are in not-ok position, but consistently try to prove that they are in ok position by attacking and controlling others. Though they are week from inside but they try to overcome their weaknesses through their aggressiveness and try to emulate strengths with their rude behaviour.

Assertive Behaviour

Assertive behaviour is considered the most effective for leadership. Assertive people ask for what they want, say what they believe, and standup for their rights in a way that others can accept. The quality of assertiveness means being straightforward yet open to the needs of others. Assertiveness strikes the correct balance being too dominant and too soft, which is an effective way to influence others.

Assertiveness is a process of expressing thoughts and feelings while asking for what one wants in an appropriate ways without jeopardizing the rights and dignity of others. These persons stand up to their rights without violating the rights of others.

Non-verbal communication of assertive person includes the facial expression like smiling, eye contact, pleasant voice, erect postures and firm gesture. The person with assertive behaviour is having the self-concepts. They do not get threatened and do not allow others to control their behaviour. The assertive behaviour is considered the most effective for leaders.

SPIRITUALITY

Spirituality provides an insight into the nature of consciousness and has a universal appeal. It has the best of religion, philosophy and science and has appeal for the theist, atheist and non-believers too. It messages for love, kindness and purity. Spirituality inspires people for their individual liberation from evils and the resultant sufferings and equips them with the knowledge and spiritual power that can satisfactorily fulfil their social obligation and family duties and helps them to attain excellence and transcendental perfection.

Spiritual dimensions are dreadfully needed in leadership dynamics to overcome existing chronic crises of people. Though there are various views regarding spirituality all over the world and people perceive different meanings of spirituality based on their culture, religion and lifestyle. But we have taken the spiritualistic approach based on ancient Indian scriptures. Following are the spiritual thoughts engrossed in ancient Indian scripture Bhagavad Gita compiled and translated by Prabhupada (2003).

Generating Excellence in Work

A popular verse of the Bhagavad Gita advises "detachment" from the results of actions performed in the course of one's duty. Being dedicated to work has to mean "working for the sake of work, generating excellence for its own sake." If we are always calculating the earnings and expecting the recognition and rewards before and after putting in our efforts, then such work is not detached. It is not "generating excellence for its own sake", but working only for the extrinsic reward that may or may not result. So the Bhagavad Gita tells us that we should not mortgage our efforts for uncertain future. Thus, the best means of effective performance management is the working itself. Attaining this state of mind (called "Nishkaam Karma" means working without any expectations of future gains) is the right attitude to work because it prevents the ego, the mind from dissipation of attention through speculation on future gains or losses. We must seek pleasure and generate inspiration from work itself and not from consequences in terms of recognition and rewards. "Work is worship". Excellence in karma (work) is the highest form of yoga.

In Bhagavad Gita the Lord Krishna told to his disciple Arjuna that take action—not for your own benefit, not for satisfying your own greed and desire, but for the good of many, with faith in the ultimate victory of ethics over unethical actions and of truth over untruth. It could be taken to mean doing something because it is worthwhile, to serve others, to make the world a better place. He further added that you have right to perform your duty, but you are not entitled to the fruits of action. Never consider yourself the cause of the results of your activities, and never be attached to not doing your duty. Be free from all dualities and from all anxieties for gain and safety, and be established in the self. Perform your duty equipoise. Abandoning all the attachments to success or failure, it will help you to achieve equability means calm state of mind where you do not become angry or upset, especially in difficult situations. Such composure is called **yoga**. Yoga means to concentrate the mind upon the supreme by controlling the ever-disturbing senses. The anxiety is the product of expectations; if you want to overcome anxiety, get detached from expectations of future gains and losses.

Undetached work causes bondage in this material world and detachment will always keep you free from bondage.

The concentration on work (with ethics in work) without future speculations of personal gains provides us the calmness. The calm mind in the face of failure will lead to deeper introspection and observe evidently where the process went wrong so that corrective steps could be taken in future course of action.

My imperfections and failures are as much a blessing from God as my successes and my talents and I lay them both at his feet; Action may not always bring happiness, but there is no happiness without action (Mahatma Gandhi quotes).

According to Lord Krishna, "he who generates wealth after serving the people, through work done as a sacrifice for them and with an intention to contribute, is liberated from all sins. On the other hand, those earn wealth only for themselves with an intention to serve their greed and desires, without ethics in work, eat sins and leads to frustration and failure."

Implications of detachment on performance

The model shown in Figure 16.4 depicts very clearly that if we concentrate more on our gains, rewards, and promotions, etc. we involve ourselves in speculation of future gains and losses and this creates mental stress, which forms a thick sheet over our unconscious mind and produce blockage between unconscious and conscious mind. Our conscious mind does not work in coordination with unconscious mind and our attention from the work get dissipated that result into poor performance.

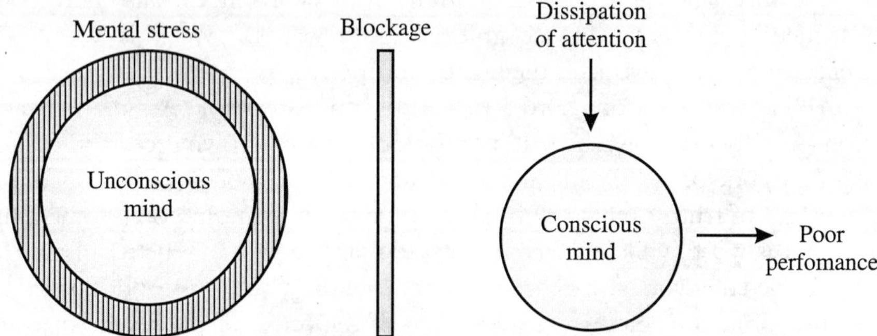

Figure 16.4 Concerned for future gains and losses.

The model shown in Figure 16.5 indicates that the detachment from the futures gains and losses and concentration on work to generate excellence for its own sake, create positive energy, which allows free flow between unconscious and conscious mind. The concentration on performance increases and generates miraculous performance.

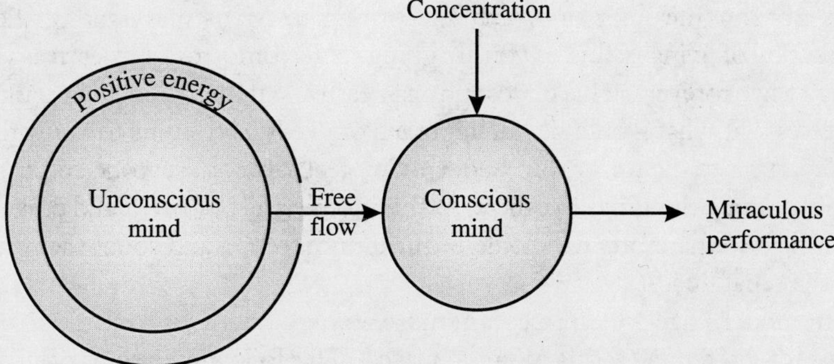

Figure 16.5 Detachment from future gains and losses.

Thus, the best means of effective performance and generating excellence in work is getting detached form future consequences and working for work itself. Attaining this state of mind (called "Nishkaam Karma") is the right attitude to work because it prevents the ego, and dissipation of attention through speculation of future gains and losses.

Contribution

Thinking for our needs and possessions and to satisfy them is putting us into endless cycle. The satisfaction becomes delusion as there is no end to our personal desires and as soon as our one need is fulfilled, another comes in front immediately. This particular need based thinking build our attitude of searching the meaning of the world for us. When we do not find meaning in people or situation with regard to our needs, they become meaningless for us. The highest level of frustration arises when the whole world become meaningless for us.

The modern psychologists have identified various primary human needs and tried to arrange them in order, but as described above actually all these needs are delusive symptoms and its satisfaction is leading us toward meaninglessness.

The right approach of generating satisfaction is to develop a sense of contribution. We must think about meaning of our existence. How we can find the meaning of our life? How we can make ourselves meaningful to others? The search for various ways to contribute, to sacrifice for others and action to make ourselves more meaningful, provides highest level of satisfaction. If you are achieving personal success in terms of getting promotions, money, or possessions, your happiness would at best be shared by only your close friends and family members for a very short period of time and then everything will become meaningless. But if you contribute in the achievement of societal needs or in generating wealth for society, sacrifice your own needs for others then the whole society will share your success and you will always feel satisfied as you will carry a sense of your meaning or worth. According to Mahatma Gandhi, the core philosophy of living is "live as you are going to die tomorrow and learn as you are going to live forever". This philosophy can easily be understood by just asking to ourselves that what would be our approach or deeds if we come to know that we are departing to die tomorrow. Suddenly we feel love for everyone and trying to distribute our belongings to others. At this moment all our needs and desires turn into ashes. So therefore, we should begin at once to live, and count each separate day as a separate life.

In modern age we cannot learn more about a "sense of contribution" than from Mother Teresa (Mother Teresa quotes). Her following quotes provide us a sense of contribution:

- Let us not be satisfied with just giving money. Money is not enough, money can be got, but they need your hearts to love them. So, spread your love everywhere you go.
- I do not claim anything of the work. It is his work. I am like a little pencil in his hand. That is all. He does the thinking. He does the writing. The pencil has nothing to do with it.
- I see God in every human being. When I wash the leper's wounds, I feel I am nursing the Lord himself. Is it not a beautiful experience?
- No matter who says what, you should accept it with a smile and do your own work.

Integration

The spiritual integration suggests that all living beings in the world are same and have the light of God. The teachings of Lord Buddha tells us that in the sky, there is no distinction of east and west; people create distinctions out of their own minds and then blasé them to be true. Life is dear to all beings; they have the right to live the same as we do. We are the same as plants, as trees, as other people, as the rain that falls. We consist of that which is around us; we are the same as everything.

We should have a "sense of relationship" means we have definite relationship with all the creatures of the world, so it is immaterial to define the purpose for relationship before building it.

Immature love says: "I love you because I need you." Mature love says: "I need you because I love you." (Buddhist Saying)

Three Modes of Material Nature

There are three modes of material nature—lunacy, obsession, and graciousness.

Mode of lunacy

The mode of lunacy is born of ignorance, is the delusion of all embodied living entities. The results of this mode are madness, indolence, sleep, foolishness and illusion. The persons who are in the mode of lunacy appear to be always dejected and are addicted to intoxicants and sleeping. Whatever they do is neither good for them nor for anyone. When there is no illumination, knowledge is absent. One in the mode of lunacy acts whimsically, for no purpose. Even though he has the capacity to work, he makes no endeavour. This is called **illusion**. Although consciousness is going on, life is inactive. In the mode of lunacy people become mad. Being distressed by their circumstances they take shelter of intoxication, and thus, they sink further into ignorance. Their future life is very dark.

Mode of obsession

The mode of obsession is a born of unlimited desires and longings. When this mode of material nature increased, one develops the hankering for material enjoyment. He wants to enjoy sense gratification means honour in the society, or in the nation, he wants nice wife, children, house and other luxuries. To achieve his endless desires of pleasing his wife, children, society, and to keep up his prestige, one has to work very hard. Therefore, the whole material world is more or less in the mode of obsession. Modern civilization is considered to be advanced in the standard of mode of obsession. In the mode of obsession, people become greedy, and their hankering for sense enjoyment has no limit. One can see that even if one has enough money and adequate arrangements for sense gratification, there is neither happiness nor peace of mind.

The action in the mode of obsession results in misery. Personal desires, egoism, delusion, absence of commitment to service, personal gains, give and take relationships, and love with a string of expectations; arrogance; conceit; anger; harshness and ignorance exists in people who are in deep mode of obsession. People of obsessive nature are arrogant, carrying proud in possessing some type of education or so much wealth. They desire to be worshipped by others, and demand respectability, although they do not command respect. Over trifles they become very angry and speak harshly, not gently. They do everything whimsically, according to their own desire, and they do not recognize any authority. They are fully trapped in personal needs, desires and lust. They lose their intelligence in fulfilling their endless desires; the whole world becomes meaningless for them. They engage in unbeneficial, horrible works meant to destroy the world. They say that they mean business and they are professional. In fact, they are professional destroyers. Though with their passion towards fulfilling their needs they produce efficiency but mere efficiency, in the work is not enough to generate satisfaction, efficiency with right intentions is important.

Mode of graciousness

If one wants happiness at all, his money and possessions will not help him; he has to elevate himself to the mode of graciousness through relentless learning and quest for knowledge.

The mode of graciousness, being purer than the others, is illuminating, and it frees one from all sinful reactions. Those situated in that mode become conditioned by a sense of happiness and knowledge. A man in this mode is not so much affected by material miseries, and he has a sense of advancement in material knowledge. In Vedic literature, it is said that the mode of graciousness means greater knowledge and a greater sense of happiness. The quest for knowledge in the mode of graciousness is not to become more knowledgeable person than others or to gain honour from society or nation, rather it is for giving services to people, contributing effectively for betterment of the society and engendering peace and harmony in the planet. A gracious person is satisfied by generating excellence in his work or intellectual pursuit. He can see things as they are. The mode of graciousness develops knowledge, sense of contribution, sense of service, devotion towards spiritual master (Lord Krishna), integrity, and detachment from the fruits of actions. Thus, the action under mode of graciousness results in purity, satisfaction, and peace of mind.

To become an effective leader you must incur important spiritual dimensions into your paradigm. The spiritual thinking will provide true guidance to define one's mission, roles, goals, and values. It will help one to reach in a mode of graciousness. By being in a mode of graciousness you may be able to understand more clearly about how satisfaction and peace of mind can be attained and you can achieve self-transcendence state.

EMOTIONAL RECIPROCATION

As a leader you need to develop and maintain productive relationships with people in your internal and external work environment. These people may be your subordinates, superiors, colleagues, customers, dealers, suppliers, and even friends. For a world-class leader knowledge of people is more important than product knowledge. Treat people with respect on your way up because you will be meeting them on your way down. True relationships are the platforms on which all leadership roles can be performed. True relationship with people around you provides people victory. The objectives of true relationship is not only to have good talking terms or to eat lunch together; it is actually about building emotional bonds with people, developing trust, increasing effectiveness, developing synergy, and generating satisfaction in the work environment. To develop true relationships with people, you need to work sincerely on the model of emotional reciprocation given in Figure 16.6.

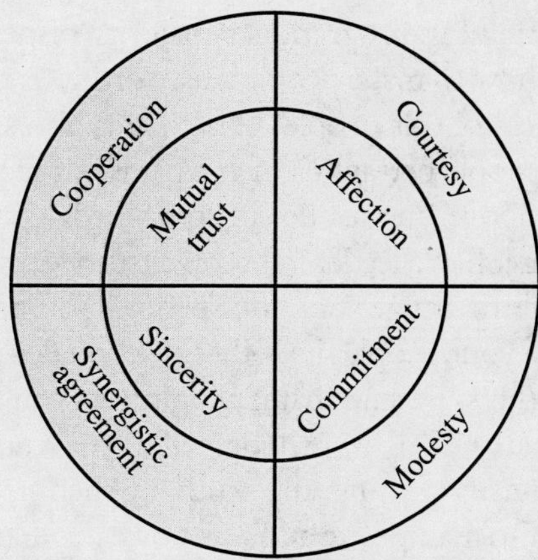

Figure 16.6 Dimensions of emotional reciprocation.

Majority of managers in their leadership role fails to develop good and productive relations with people because they jump directly into developing interpersonal relationship without working on their own personal paradigms. In other words, they go for people victory without achieving personal victory, whereas personal victory is the prerequisite for people victory or a person must work on emotional autonomy model to become emotionally independent and then go for emotional reciprocation model. We are living in interdependent world. People are interdependent to each other. To have productive interdependency you need to be emotionally independent first. Emotionally independent means free from greed, environmental influences, concern for future gains and losses, and the influences of other's weaknesses. This emotional independence can be achieved only through developing your personal paradigm.

The emotional reciprocation model shown in Figure 16.6 suggests that to win people's heart and to develop productive relationship with all stakeholders in business you need to work on various dimensions ranging from mutual trust to building synergistic agreement. We will discuss each dimension in detail here.

MUTUAL TRUST

It takes very long time with patient efforts to win trust of others, but takes only a moment to lose it. The hardest work in the world is to get back the trust of others after losing it.

True relationships demand mutual trust. The trust is emotional glue that binds the followers and the leader together. The lack of trust creates stress, barrier to communication, non-cooperation, suspicion and loss of productivity at the workplace. Developing trust in the environment is one of the major jobs a leader has to perform. The mutual trust provides us a platform to build synergy in the environment, i.e., true interdependence and profound respect for each other.

In our leadership training programmes majority of participants ask about how to build trust and how to make people trustworthy? Is there any measure to assess the trustworthiness of our people? Participants also say that we trust our people but if the same people betrays us then what is our fault.

The answer to all above queries lies in two words that are "become" and "trustworthy". It is your job as a leader to become trustworthy for your people. It is you who have to pull the trigger not your people. You need to be believable, credible, and truthful to your people first otherwise you do not deserve to expect trustworthiness from others. Be sure that if people trust you they are trustworthy and if they do not, they are not. Trust includes telling the truth but it goes beyond just not lying. This means putting the truth in such a way that it can be misinterpreted. In order to manipulate and seek power from the system most of us do this mistake and lose the trust of our people.

How to Become Trustworthy?

Be credible

To win the trust you need to be credible to your followers. Credibility is earned hour-by-hour, day-by-day, year-by-year over time and can be lost in an instant. To earn credibility clarify your values, talk to your followers and tell them what is important to you and what is not, identify your followers' needs and build consensus, be sincere with them, stand up for your belief and lead by examples. There are some do nots that you have to follow strictly that are as hereunder:

- Do not criticize people on their back.
- Do not let your people down at their vulnerable time.
- Do not hurt other's emotions. To a sadist everything is funny as long as it is happening to someone else. Remember, "an injury is forgiven more easily than an insult."
- Do not use position power and authority deceptively in relationship.
- Do not call for written explanations instead prefer face-to-face interaction.
- Do not say yes to create good image. Learn to say no for wrong things.
- Do not try to be nice person. Try to be right person.

Be willing to be influenced by others

Most of the managers in present time possess this common lacuna in their personality that they scare of getting influenced by others. That is why, they listen to people only to give answers and not to understand others emotions and in the process they become icy, rigid and good talker. They avoid eye-to-eye contact and use memos and written reports.

Real leaders are good listeners and always want to understand people's emotions and to be influenced by others. They view listening as learning opportunity and as a tool to build trust. They use empathy to understand other's feelings and are not scared of loosing control over others or to getting influenced by others. They always ask people "come and talk to me, influence me".

Be open and share information

Good leaders are transparent, open for discussions, and are willing to share information with their subordinates. Your openness allows people to come closer to you and share their feelings and that makes the foundation for building mutual trust.

Be compassionate

You should be considerate for your people by being sensitive for their emotions, feelings and afflictions. Leaders think about their people before themselves. They have caring attitude towards their people. They take the responsibility for satisfaction, growth, development, and quality life of their subordinates.

Mere sympathy with others' afflictions and weaknesses is not enough to build trust. You need to develop desire to help others to overcome their problems and weaknesses. When people are in problem, your willing help can build high trust in your relationships.

Emotional condensation

Emotional condensation is related to emotional deposits in the hearts of others. If we do something good for people, keep commitments, and perform small courtesies with them, everything is deposited in the form of positive emotions in their heart. If we scold people, shout on them, betray commitment, and hurt their emotions through our misconduct, we actually make withdrawal of emotions from their heart.

This is a continuous process in human interactions and as a leader you must always try to condense emotional reservoir in the heart of people. No matter how much you have helped some one in the past but if your emotional deposit is nil or in minus because of your withdrawals, your relationship with a person would always be at the verge of splitting.

To condense your emotional reservoir in the people's heart, you need to understand them, listen to them patiently and empathically, be courteous and attend to little things, keep your commitment, and help them passionately whenever they require. Do not undermine the importance of apologizing sincerely whenever you make any withdrawal.

Showing integrity with your people is also very important. You must defend your people when they not present. By doing this, you can make huge emotional deposits not only in the hearts of those you are defending but also, in the heart of persons present.

In the interpersonal relationship, it is vital to clarify each other's expectations. Normally we have seen that in relationships people start expecting more and more without communicating to each other, and they come to a point when expectations are not fulfilled, the process of emotional withdrawals begin and an emotional reserve comes down to break even point or even below.

Respect for each other's beliefs

All the individuals possess their own belief systems and perceptions that they learn from their culture, society, social groups and families. We normally try to impose our beliefs, our way of life, and perceptions on others and want them to respect and believe the same. In fact, this is the major cause behind all the differences and lack of trust between the religions and communities in the world. We need to be enough broadminded or be able to detach ourselves from our cultural, regional, and religious biases so that in true sense we can appreciate other's beliefs and generate wisdom to discriminate between what is good and what is bad.

AFFECTION

Affection is, for many, the essential cement of a relationship. Without it, many feel totally alienated. With it, they become emotionally bonded. You feel terrific when your friend is affectionate, and you feel terrible when there is not enough of it, you have the emotional need for affection.

Affection is the expression of care. It symbolizes security, protection, comfort and approval which are the vital ingredients in any relationship. When one person is affectionate toward the other, the following messages are sent:

- You are important to me. I will care for you and protect you.
- I am concerned about the problems you face and will be there for you whenever you need me.
- I need you because I love you.

Affection is something that flows among people, something that one gives and one receives. Affection allows people to maintain each other's dignity. It is not bounded by a string of give and take rather it engender sacrifice for each other. To be affectionate listen to your mind some of the time, and your **heart** all the time. Look people in the eye and smile sincerely. Be kind to others as kindness is a language the deaf can hear and blind can see.

COMMITMENT

As true as this is for the success of a corporation, it is even more so for the individual. The most important single factor in individual success is **commitment.** Commitment helps in bringing emotional involvement and alignment. To commit is to promise yourself for a certain purpose or line of conduct. It also means practicing your beliefs consistently. There are, therefore, two fundamental conditions for commitment. The first is having a sound set of beliefs. There is an old saying that goes, "stand for something or you will fall for anything." The second is faithful adherence to those beliefs with your behaviour. Possibly the best description of commitment is "persistence with a purpose". Commitment says:

- I am willing to sacrifice for you because I care.
- I am a person of integrity you can trust me.
- I will not let you down in your good or bad times.
- Despite pain I will always be there with you.
- I do not have any expectation.

SINCERITY

Sincerity is the virtue of one who speaks truly about his or her own feelings, thoughts, and desires. It reflects your truthful intentions.

You need to be sincere towards your people. When your people are in trouble you must be there to help them. In the present time, most of us in a leadership role pretend to be sincere towards our followers but in reality we seldom have any emotions for them. As a world-class leader you should stay away from pretense. Do not ask your subordinates to what you can do for them, instead be there with them and do whatever you can, in your capacity. Stay away from meaningless and phony pleasantries and offer your help or assistance before it is asked.

COOPERATION

Cooperation is a process of working or acting together in harmony to produce great results. The aim of developing synergy in the environment can be achieved by developing creative cooperation in the relationships and work environment.

In any relationship when there is creative cooperation among individuals, synergy develops in the environment. Developing synergy in the environment is one of the most important tasks of a leader. The common ingredients of creative cooperation are mutual trust, consideration, creative compromise and respect for differences.

When trust is high, people considers each other's problems and respect each other's differences, the creative compromise takes place. People sacrificing their expectations for each other and sharing their benefits with each other are actually compromising with each other. As shown in Figure 16.7, this compromise becomes creative when persons involved in an interaction are bending towards each other at the same angle in upward directions. They form an apex and embrace each other's differences, experiences, knowledge and skills to create

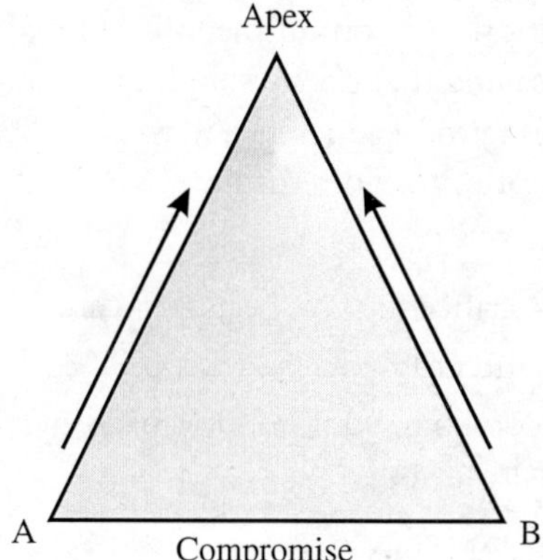

Figure 16.7 Creative compromise.

some amazing new things. This is actually the peak of synergistic environment where world-class performances are visualized.

COURTESY

Think about the situation when you wanted to cross the road, but you are prevented from doing so from the heavy traffic. How did you feel when someone recognizing your problem slowed down, waved to you, and let you crossed the road? Your frustration was instantly transformed into relief and thankfulness.

Courtesy means showing respects and kindness to others. A courteous person, who is not very sharp, will go farther in life than a discourteous but sharp person. It helps tremendously in winning the heart and trust of others.

How are we to practice courtesy? There are many moments in a day when you encounter with people. Every encounter is an opportunity. Here are some examples:

- Whenever someone treats you kindly, show your appreciation, express your gratitude, and offer your sincere thanks.
- Give sincere smile when you meet others. Remember, smile is a curved line that can straighten many problems.
- Recognize the achievements of others, not with shallow flattery, but with sincere and warm praise.
- Respect the opinions and decisions of others even if you disagree with them.
- Be a good friend.
- Treat everyone with respect regardless of their positions.
- Respond to rudeness with kindness.
- Never underestimate the power of your small acts of kindness. They are pebbles which form a solid foundation for our civilization.

MODESTY

One who lives and behaves in simplicity quietly performs daily tasks and routines without the trumpet blown before. There is no need to call attention. Modesty acts gently, but with no less perfection or care as one who may constantly announce their deeds.

Modest people do not talk much about their achievements, capabilities and greatness. They are simple and grounded. They do not hurt other's emotions and respect differences. They appreciate other's viewpoints even if they are not agreeing to them. They are peace-makers; their presence brings peace in the environment.

SYNERGISTIC AGREEMENT

We are living in interdependent world and whenever two persons or a group of people develop any working relationship they get involved in some kind of agreement where expectations of all the persons involved are clarified.

Synergistic agreement is, what is required between individuals whenever they get involved in working relationships. This agreement is all about developing harmony and creating synergy in the interpersonal relationships. Synergistic agreement is the mindset of people involved in the relationship suggesting about the mutual benefits. In other words, benefits generated by people must be shared equally. There should not be any winner or loser in the environment. No one should be benefited at the cost of others.

Synergistic agreements between leaders and followers, sales persons and customers are developed on two basic dimensions that are empathy and assertion shown in Figure 16.8.

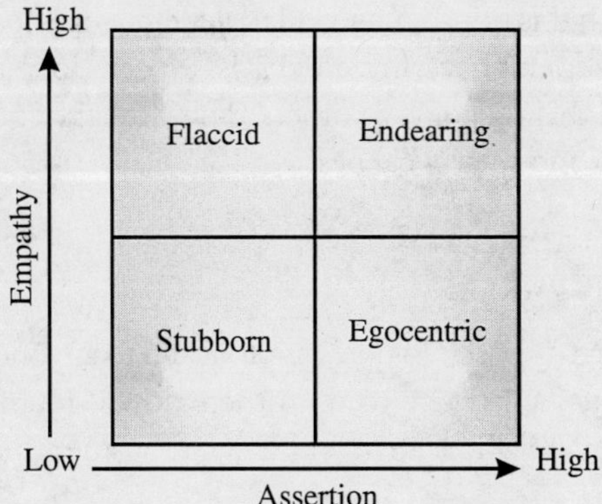

Figure 16.8 Synergistic agreement.

Empathy is the skill that is utilized to understand another person's emotions, feelings, expectations and state of mind. To understand other's emotions one need to use empathic listening. Empathic listening is listening through eyes and heart along with the ears. Through ears we listen to words, through eyes we understand the body language and facial expressions, and by the heart we understand the emotions. Persons who listen without empathy actually listen just to give reply or to listen what they want to listen, and in the process they filter everything through their own goggles.

Assertion is expressing your opinion and desires strongly and with confidence so that people take notice. To make synergistic agreement understanding other's expectations is important but at the same time putting your expectations is also important. With the combinations of high and low level of both the dimensions, there exist four kinds of mindsets of human interactions, namely egocentric, flaccid, stubborn and synergistic mindsets.

Egocentric Mindset

A person with egocentric mindset tries to get maximum benefits out of any relationship. He becomes selfish in his attitude and does not want to see other's interest. He concentrates only on his own interest. This type of mindset create low trust situation in the environment. In this kind of mindset, people become highly assertive or aggressive and lack empathy in their behaviour. They lose their interest to understand other's emotions or problems.

Flaccid Mindset

Persons with flaccid mindset are extremely passive in nature. They always try to be nice person and not to be a right person. They go along to get along with people. Any interaction with this mindset will fail to generate harmony and synergy in the environment. They do not have any standards, expectations and vision. People are ready to sacrifice all their benefits to others. They lose the courage to express their feelings and start loving their weaknesses.

Stubborn Mindset

People with stubborn mindset do not want to listen to anyone. They become blind to everything except their desire to put others down. Human interactions with this mindset destroy the whole environment and business may not last for long.

Synergistic Mindset

As a leader you must keep synergistic mindset in your interactions with people. This mindset forms the base for synergistic agreements described earlier. Leaders with synergistic mindset consider others' benefits and at the same time consider the organizations' benefits too. They make an attempt to create harmony and satisfaction in the environment so that each person should come out as a winner. This mindset fosters the level of mutual trust, cooperation to the maximum. The principle of creative cooperation actually visualized at the attainment of synergistic mindset.

17

Tips to Improve Interpersonal Skills

Working on emotional reciprocation model and bringing all its dimensions to your character is important to build long-term relationships with people, but along with this you need to work also on some interpersonal behavioural skills to reflect truly what is inside you. Try these following tips to improve your interpersonal skills:

Smile

Remember smile is that small curved line which can straighten many complex problems. It is also very important tool to keep you always calm and exuberant. Smile often. The positive energy you radiate will draw others to you.

Pay attention to others

Acknowledge sincerely and congratulate people for their achievements, and show your happiness in others' happy moments. Express concern and sympathy for the difficult situations such as an illness or death. Make eye contact and address people by their first names. Ask others for their opinions.

Practice empathic listening

To actively listen is to demonstrate that you intend to hear and understand others' point of view. It means restating in your own words, what the other person has said. In this way, you know that you understood their meaning and they know that your responses are more than lip service. Your co-workers will appreciate knowing that you really do listen to what they have to say.

Appreciate others

Find one positive thing about everyone you work with and let them hear it. Be generous with praise and kind words of encouragement. Say 'thank you' when someone helps you. Make colleagues feel welcome when they call or stop by your office. If you let others know that they are appreciated, they all want to give you their best.

Be a mediator

Take a step beyond simply bringing people together, and become someone who resolves conflicts when they arise. Learn how to be an effective mediator. If co-workers argue over personal or professional disagreements, arrange to sit down with both parties and help to sort out their differences. By taking on such a leadership role, you will garner respect and admiration from those around you.

Build cohesive environment

Create an environment that encourages others to work together. Treat everyone equally, and do not play favourites. Avoid talking about others behind their backs. Follow-up on other people's suggestions or requests. When you make a statement or announcement, check to see that you have been understood. If people see you as someone solid and fair, they will grow to trust you.

Be humourous

Use humour to make atmosphere lighter and break communication barriers between you and others. Do not be skeptical to joke on yourself. You will gain others' affection.

18

Vitality of Relationships

Herminia Ibarra (2008), Professor of Organizational Behaviour says that many leaders today make potentially fatal career mistake of giving less priority to building relationships with diverse group of people in comparison to other job responsibilities. She says that what you know is who you know and insists that network of people is extremely vital for business leaders in today's competitive environment.

There are three type of network of people important in business: operational, personal and strategic. Many leaders excel at building operational relationships with people and overlook their personal and strategic networks. By doing this they ensure to be in the same level of competencies as of their colleagues.

Operational networking involves cultivating the relationships with people you need to accomplish your job. This may mean developing relationships with your pears, seniors, subordinates and people of other departments, customers, suppliers, and channel members to win support for your initiatives and accomplish the tasks effectively. You need to have this network to get things done.

Personal relationships with diverse group of like minded professionals are very important if you really want to make your career move. But this kind of networking is a postscript for many leaders today. These networks allow you to develop important social skills. These relationships are not closely tide with your job, so you can not feel its importance tangibly in performing your job. But these contacts allow you to develop professionally, your personality, and emotional acumen on the whole. Personal network provide you the edge over your pears by inducing dynamism and confidence in your personality. As some great person told once that you tell me about your friends I will tell you what kind of person you are.

Strategic networking is toughest but most essential for business leaders. It encourages you to look beyond your industry. These relationships allow you to learn different management practices, leadership approaches, utilization of technologies in different industries. This also helps leaders to see bigger picture and create their own visionary approach.

According to Ibarra all types of above described networks make huge difference in leadership. This is where strategic ideas come into play. This is what allows people to line up stakeholders. In actual practice, this is the area where most people have serious gap.

As a leader you need to develop two way relationships with people. If you pick up the phone only when you are in crises then you may not go very long with your relations. You need to extend your hands in others' crises too.

Relationships take time, they take efforts and they have their own rhythm so be patient and utilize your emotional reciprocation acumen described earlier. Depending on what you put into your relationships, what you give back to it and to the extent you are investing for future, your network will be there for you. When you look at what top companies do as they try to assess the leaders they currently have, they will tell you very clearly that the ability to manage relationships across boundaries and to sell ideas is a critical competency.

19

Development of Good Habits

We are what we repeatedly do unconsciously. Anything we do repeatedly stabilize in our unconscious mind and becomes a habit. Anything we do consciously is not a habit.

HABITS

If we are doing same things repeatedly for number of times, then actually we are conditioning our unconscious mind. Most of our behaviour comes as a result of conditioning. In a position of a leader, it is your responsibility to condition your unconscious mind in a positive manner and bring all the acumens in your unconscious competence. Good habits are tough to come, but easy to live with. Bad habits come easily but are tough to live with.

Acquiring Leadership Competences as Habits

Acquiring leadership competence in your habit typically involves progress through four stages, which are illustrated in Figure 19.1. When you start reading this book you do not know what you do not know. This is actually the **stage-1** known as unconscious incompetence. This means people are unaware of their incompetence. They lack leadership competence, probably because they have never tried to be a leader or to know about leadership competences before. By reading this book or taking lessons from a trainer you become conscious of what is required, to do well as a leader and you come to know that you do not possess the same. In other words, you become conscious about your incompetence. This is the **stage-2** known as conscious incompetence where you can learn about leadership processes for instance, creating a vision, building a team, etc. The **stage-3** is conscious competence in which you consciously start practicing leadership behaviour. You learn to visualize a desired future, influence others to engage in that future, and have the courage to take on real change. You receive positive feedback from your skills and actions, and are aware of how well you are doing, which sets up the transition into **stage-4**. In the stage four due to repetition of behaviour in stage-3, your skills and behaviour conditions your unconscious and your skills become a part of you. They occur naturally as your habit. You no longer consciously think about leadership behaviour; it emerges automatically in your habit.

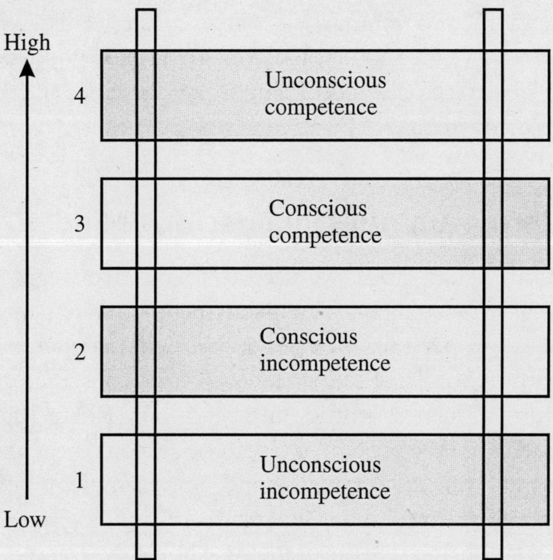

Figure 19.1 Competence ladder.

If you have ever heard the argument that 'leaders are born rather than made', or that someone is a natural leader, it would mean that they operate in stage-4 without having to go through the first three stages. But this is rare. Most of us have to struggle to get awareness of what leadership is about and then become competent through practice and experience. This book helps people achieve stages-2 and -3 in their progress towards becoming a leader. The chapters develop your cognitive understanding of what leaders be, know and do. You can build competence by contemplating on your understanding acquired through this book, and applying these concepts in actual business settings, in your relationships with others, in social groups, in voluntary organizations, and even with friends and family.

How to Develop Good Habits?

A large portion of our brain is covered by unconscious mind. It accepts inputs without the distinction of good or bad and positive or negative. We do not even have power to stop any information to go to our unconscious. Whatever we experience, listen, observe, see and speak every moment, are directly going and storing in our unconscious mind. Our habits are the reflection of the state and conditioning of our unconscious mind. In fact, we are constantly being conditioned, consciously or unconsciously, by exposure to the kind of books we read, movies and TV programmes we watch, music we listen to, company we keep, and statement we give about ourselves. To develop good habits and to drop bad habits, we have to actually reprogram our unconscious and reach to the stage of unconscious competence.

Tips to Reprogram our Unconscious Mind

To reprogram our unconscious, we need to follow two stages. In stage-1; you must make use of self-statements. A self-statement is a statement made in present tense, of the kind of person you want to be. Self-statements are like writing commercial about you. They influence both your conscious and unconscious mind that, in turn, influences attitude and behaviour (Khera 2002).

Self-statements are the process of repetition. If you repeat a statement several times, it sinks into your unconscious mind. For example, if you repeatedly tell yourself, "I am assertive," you will start responding assertively in your interpersonal relationships. Self-statements should be framed in positive way because we think in pictures, not in words, and we want to create positive picture in our mind of what we want to be rather than what we do not want. Few examples of positive and negative self-statements are given in Table 19.1.

In stage-2 you visualize a mental picture of what you want to have and do, then make conscious efforts to bring your thoughts into an action. When you will perform an action repeatedly based on your positive thoughts, very soon it will come to your habit. For example, by behaving courageously we learn courage, by practicing honesty and fairness continuously we learn these traits and we master them.

TABLE 19.1 Positive Self-statements for Leaders

Positive Self-statements for Leaders
• I am cool and I can handle any situation with patience.
• I know what my life's mission is and what are my roles and goals?
• I carry positive attitude and possess high self-esteem.
• I have a sense of contribution and I believe in sacrifice rather than fulfilling my needs.
• I know my values.
• I understand that it is my responsibility to take initiatives. I can control my circumstances. I can respond consciously.
• I explore myself and try to find where I have gone wrong instead putting allegation on others.
• I am disciplined.
• I am assertive.
• I have synergistic mindset.
• I am modest.
• I strongly believe in honesty, sincerity and commitment.
• I am courteous.
• I am a leader with a vision in the organization.
• I can do mentoring.
• I can bring changes in the organization.
• I can develop world-class culture.
• I can motivate others.

Leaders' Language

To become a true leader and to bring leadership thoughts and habit to our unconscious competence, at the initial stages we must check our language and ensure that we are not following non-leader's language. We should speak leader's language consciously. Remember, people will very quickly make a judgement about you, triggered by the words you use. In Table 19.2 some examples of non-leader's and leader's language are given.

TABLE 19.2 Non-Leaders' and Leaders' Language

Non-Leaders' Language	*Leaders' Language*
"I've been really lucky." It is not down to luck. Our actions and decisions are based on careful thought, planning and hard work, not luck.	Say, **"I've worked hard to achieve this result."**
"I'll try to get your report done by Friday, if I possibly can." Remove try as it suggests you can not be relied upon.	Make a commitment and say, **"I will do it by Friday."**
"I have got so many problems; I do not know where to start." Rephrase the negative word problems	Instead use **challenge**, it will feel better.
"I have spent two hours at that seminar." Spend suggests waste, loss, exhaustion.	Rephrase and use **invest** that produces a positive return.
Reactive	*Proactive*
There is nothing I can do.	Let us look our alternatives.
That is just the way I am.	I can choose a different approach.
He makes me so mad.	I control my own feelings.
He will not allow that.	I can create an effective presentation.
I have to do that.	I will choose an appropriate response.
I cannot, that is me.	Let us look at what we can do.
I have to do it.	I prefer to do it.
If only I had the boss who is more generous.	I can be more flexible and cooperative.
If I had a better position in the organization.	I can be more innovative and sincere.
Negative Approach	*Positive Approach*
I do not agree with your point.	Your point seems interesting.
You have given foolish idea.	Interesting idea.
This cannot be done.	Let us find what can be done.
Uses will not which is word of withdrawal.	Uses **did** which is word of accomplishment
Uses cannot which is word of defeat.	Uses **can** which is a word of authority.

Finally, working very sincerely on various dimensions discussed in this section will provide you wonderful success in your life and you would be able to enjoy the status of world class leader. A person who is organizational builder and who has the capacity to transform average organization into world-class organization through successful implementation of leadership approaches.

SECTION III

COURSE OF ACTION

20

Leadership Functions

Figure 20.1 shows different functions that leaders need to perform at the work place during their course of action. One of the foremost functions of leaders is to challenge the existing system and create a distant picture of the organization

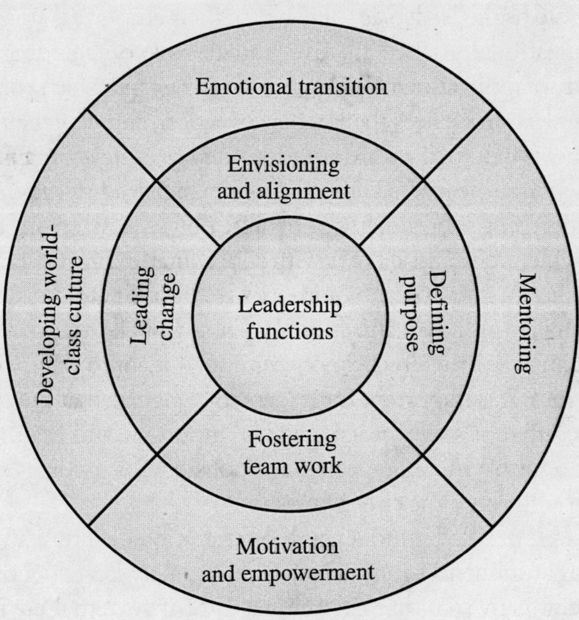

Figure 20.1 Leadership functions.

or of their respective unit. They align people with their vision and make everyone as stakeholder of the vision. They provide direction to their unit or to the whole organization.

In the organization, employees are generally at four emotional stages that are, denial stage, resistance stage, exploration stage, and commitment stage. The leaders' job is to bring everyone into commitment stage where everyone is committed to the organization. This process of bringing people from denial stage to commitment stage is known as **emotional transition**.

Detecting and defining the purpose of the organization is one of the important functions that a leader has to perform. Leaders provide all the information to their employees and ask them to participate in detecting the mission of the organization. This mission provides the focus and meaning to employees.

As discussed earlier, that everyone of us have tremendous potential but in most of us the major percentage of our potential is in dormant state. The leaders' job is to take out the potentials of their employees, develop and customize them with organizational and environmental needs through the process of mentoring and teaching.

Developing teamwork is such an important leadership function that team building is said to differentiate successful from unsuccessful leaders. A challenge faced by leaders studying subject of teamwork is that the words team and teamwork are overused. For some of the people, team is simply another term for a group. But only real teams can make high performance organizations.

Another role of the leaders is to motivate their employees to make efforts to achieve organizational goals. Effective leaders have outstanding inspirational skills. The study of motivation helps leaders to understand what prompts people to initiate action, what influences their choice of action, and why they persist in that action overtime. When workers are not motivated to achieve organizational goals, the fault is often in the leaders. The one way in which leaders can meet the higher motivational needs of subordinates is to shift power down from the top of the organizational hierarchy and share it with subordinates. Empowerment is power sharing, the delegation of power or authority to subordinates in the organization.

A major change in the organization does not happen easily. However, leaders do facilitate change and thereby help organizations adapt to external environment and opportunities. It is important for leaders to recognize that the change process goes through different stages, each stage is important and each may require a significant amount of time. Leaders are responsible for guiding employees and the organization through the change process.

Leaders align people by influencing organizational culture and shaping the environment that influences morale and performance. Leaders now understand that when a company's culture fits the needs of its external environment and company strategy, employees can generate competencies and core competencies that cannot be imitated easily by competitors.

21

Envisioning and Alignment

You can easily experience practically by thinking and planning about the future, you feel joy and can become exuberant, but if you think about past you will be depressed. Therefore, motivation can be generated by envisioning, and setting the future direction. An important part of your job as a leader is to set a course towards the future and get everyone in the organization moving in the same direction. Employee motivation and energy are crucial to the success of all organizations; the role of leadership is to focus everyone's energy on the same path. Many so-called managers in the corporate world feel that leadership is all about developing friendship with subordinates and influencing them to do the job, but this is just the salesmanship. The real leaders lift the vision of their employees and take them to a destination which they have never thought of.

The complexity of the environment and the uncertainty of the future are pressurizing executives to get inclined to focus on internal organizational issues where they feel they have more control. They tend to concentrate on short-term results rather then taking the long-term view. One study found that, on average, senior executives in today's organizations spend less than 3 per cent of their energy on building a corporate perspective for the future, and in some companies the average is less than 1 per cent. As a leader you need to detach yourself from bottom line working or from the trap of daily routine and look into the horizons to set the right direction for the organization and to align all the stakeholders with it.

VISION

Vision is a clear distant picture of your organization or unit that provides the direction and having a sense of destiny. Every business begins with a vision and with the hope that what is an idea today can one day become a reality. A clear vision serves as a pilot to steer the company in chosen direction. It is a guiding star, drawing everyone in the organization along the same path towards the future. When there is a genuine vision, people excel because they want to. The practice of shared vision involves the skills of unearthing shared 'pictures of the future' that foster genuine commitment and enrolment.

The legendary Jack Welch has stated that, "good business leaders create a vision, articulate a vision, passionately own the vision, and relentlessly drive the vision" (Robinson and Jack Welch 2001) .

Unless the basic concepts on which a business has been built are visible, clearly understood and explicitly expressed, the business enterprise is at the mercy of events, those events which it cannot control. Vision is not necessarily having a plan, but having a mind that always plans. As a leader you need to ensure that all the members of the organization or your unit must focus on the vision, understand and believe in achieving it.

Few examples of the visions of top companies are as follows:

Microsoft— "A personal computer on every desk in every home."

Coca-Cola— "A Coke within arm's reach of everyone on the planet".

Important Characteristics of Effective Vision

Vision must have mass appeal

The ideal vision is identified with the organization as a whole, not with a single leader or even a top leadership team. It must be able to align all the employees towards common direction and to make everyone as its stakeholder. It allows each individual to act independently, but in the same direction.

Imaginable and desirable

It must be able to convey the clear picture of what the future will look like. It should appeal to long-term interests of employees, customers, stakeholders, and others who have a stake in the enterprise. It must have emotional appeal to our fundamental needs and desires, to feel important and useful, and to believe we can make real difference in the world.

Feasible, flexible, and communicable

Vision should comprise realistic attainable goals. It must be general enough to allow individual's initiative and alternative responses in the light of changing conditions. It should be framed in easily understandable language so that it can be communicated and explained successfully. If you cannot describe your vision to someone in five minutes and draw their interest, you need to work more on the vision creation.

Power of Vision

Vision is a powerful tool to align people, to help unite a diverse workforce, and to provide them common direction. By providing direction it simplifies thousands of more detailed decisions. It energizes people and harvests their commitment. It frees people from monotony and dullness by providing them with a challenge worthy of their best efforts. A powerful vision helps the organization to achieve a bold change by involving actions and efforts of people. It provides link between today and tomorrow by working as a bridge. It motivates people to take action in the right direction, even if initial steps are personally painful. It unfolds the future events in present. Those who think and talk about present remain static and average, those who think and talk about tomorrow make their present excellent and those who think and talk about yesterday destroy their present and tomorrow.

Communicating Vision

To align people and unite diverse workforce, vision must be communicated properly. You need to ensure that vision is properly articulated and all the people concerned with the organization are the stakeholders of the same. For effective communication, you must concentrate on few elements that are as hereunder:

Simplicity

The language of the vision should be very simple and easily be understood by all the stakeholders. For the purpose eliminate all the jargons and technobabble.

Multiple forums

It must be communicated in **Multiple Forums** like big and small meetings, memos and newspapers, formal and informal interaction.

Repetition

Ideas sink in deeply only after they have been heard many times.

Leadership by example

Behaviour from top people should be consistent with the vision. Inconsistent behaviour of the top people with the vision will jeopardize other forms of communication.

Explanation of seeming inconsistencies

As a leader you must clearly explain give the reasons to people if there is any inconsistency in your behaviour with the vision. Unaddressed inconsistencies will undermine the credibility of all the communications.

Strategic Direction

The leaders who use their intuitive competence to create a vision but do not develop strategic actions to achieve the same are just a dreamer and their vision is only a fantasy and has little chance of ever becoming reality. A leader who has all action with no or little vision is a doer. He may be a hardworker and dedicated to the job and the organization, but the doer is working blind and may not truly serve the organization. The effective leaders dream big and also develop and implement strategic actions to convert their dream into reality. The vision with strategic action provides strategic direction to the organization.

"The action without vision is blind, vision without strategic action is just a fantasy, and action guided by vision is strategic direction, the hope of the organization."

To determine strategic direction for the future, leaders look inward, outward and forward. They scan both the internal and external organizational environment to identify trends, threats and the opportunities for the organization. Though some hard skills for situational analysis are required but relying too heavily on rationality can kill a vision. Overly rational people resist dreaming big. As a leader you should avoid "paralysis by analysis". Make yourself free from fear and dream big as one spiritual thought suggests that you cannot think or imagine about what does not exist in this universe. Whatever your mind can think, be sure, that is existing and you have to find it.

"Ordinary people believe only in the possible. Extraordinary people visualize not what is possible or probable, but rather what is impossible. And by visualizing the impossible, they begin to see it as possible." (Cherie Carter–Scott 1999)

22

Emotional Transition

As shown in Figure 22.1, the people are in four emotional stages in the organization, namely denial, resistance, exploration and commitment. The job of a leader is to recognize these emotional stages of each of the subordinates and respond accordingly. Let us look the characteristics of these different emotional stages.

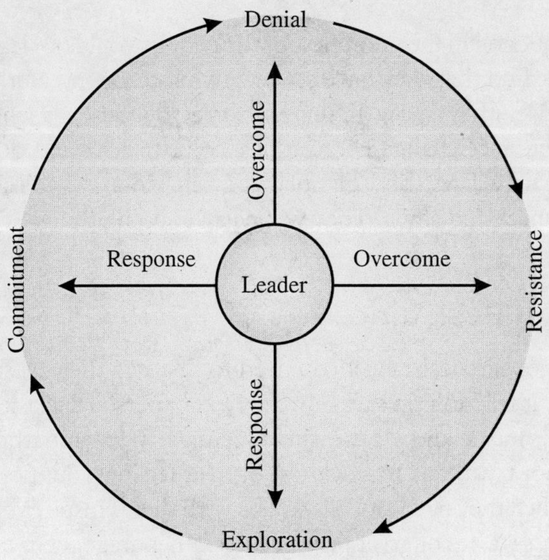

Figure 22.1 Emotional transition.

DENIAL

When employees are incompetent, highly demotivated, dissatisfied, and in a very low self-esteem state, they fall into denial stage. At this stage employees lose the interest and enthusiasm to their work. They use the language like "I do not care," and "I am not in picture", etc. They become very rigid and do not want any change either in the system or in their personal routine. They are not bothered about organization and its problems. They are sensationless towards any change. They do not want to come out of their comfort zone.

Overcoming Denial

Provide them reasons of present state of the organization and assure them that the change will take place. Communicate lots of information about the change and create a sense of urgency.

As a mentor, suggest them actions to adjust with the change and explain what to expect form the system. Show them the prevailing gaps between present state and desired state of the organization and sell the benefits of the change. Identify the hidden potential of them and communicate the same. Assure them that they are meaningful and able to take up the jobs.

Allow time to sink in. Create public problem solving climate and private safe climate to express negative feelings. Be patient for the results of your actions. Gradually with time you will find that people are moving towards resistance stage.

RESISTANCE

The drastic reduction in the numbness of the people would be clearly visible at this stage. You may find that they have started giving reactions. But because of their negative mindset they show high resistance towards any change. They are unwilling to embrace change because of insecurity, fear, and doubt. They have tremendous anxiety. They show complaining behaviour and will show their anger, and refuse to speak and smile. They will delay in doing things.

Overcoming Resistance

To overcome people's resistance, you need to first win their trust and listen very patiently to their reactions in safe climate. Do not personalize their reactions. Try to understand and acknowledge their feelings. Use empathic skills for the purpose. Do not try to talk to them out of their feelings. Support and cooperate them as and when they need, and always be with them. Inspire them by narrating them the success stories of great personalities. Encourage them to ask as many as questions. Give them the confidence about their capabilities. Generate their participation and involvement. Assure them that you will take the responsibility for negative consequences. Celebrate small wins and give all the credit to them.

EXPLORATION

This stage is characterized by people willingness to perform but they are unable to excel. The positive energy among people is clearly visible. They generate too many ideas as well as questions. People are searching for excellence and excited for learning new techniques. People at this emotional stage are disorganized, confuse and indecisive. The focus is not their.

Response to Exploration

Align them with your vision and generate their commitment with the organizational mission and goals. You need to arrange various training programmes for people to improve their skills. As a mentor, set their priorities to avoid confusion. Conduct brainstorming and planning session and ask them to develop short-term goals and objectives. This will help them to get focused. Give recognition to their ideas and reward their initiatives. Celebrate small wins. Delegate the responsibility and empower them slowly to make decisions.

COMMITMENT

People at commitment stage are organized, optimistic, goal directed, focused, and willing to accept new responsibilities. They are able to achieve excellence. They are cooperative and implement actions effectively. They are satisfied with the work environment. They have a clear sense of direction and are focused. They know their roles and expectations of management clearly.

Response to Commitment

This is the right time to implement the change. Ask your people to participate in the detecting of the mission and long-term goals of the organization. Choose committed people in the team and concentrate on the steps of team building. Look ahead and develop reward systems, motivate your subordinates intrinsically by giving them responsibility, empowering them fully to make the decisions and recognizing their achievements publicly. Create management structure to facilitate change. Establish the support system for effective performance.

23

Organizational Mission

Do your employees know why they do things they do; do they understand what they do fits into a big picture? If not does confusion often results – perhaps you do not have a mission statement. Many organizations do have a mission, few managers can tell you what is in the statement and those who can remember may not believe in the statements. F. Drucker (1992) once said:

> *"I just got the book on fourteen American companies that over several decades show nothing but superior performance. They have one thing in common: the score is clear. The mission is clear."*

The mission is very important ingredient of organizational DNA.

Mission is a broadly stated definition of the basic purpose and scope of a business. It reflects the core philosophy on which the organization is developing itself. It is the fundamental purpose that sets a firm apart from other firms of its type and identifies the scope of its operations in products and market terms. The business should be defined, not in terms of the product or service you offer, but in terms of what customer needs from your product or service to fulfill and also largely how your organization is serving the society.

The mission is made up of two critical parts: the core values and the core purpose. The core values guide the organization "no matter what." The explanation for the statement "no matter what" is that the core values embodied in our mission might be a competitive advantage, but that is not why we should have them. We should have them because they define for us what we stand for, and we should hold them even if they become a competitive disadvantage in certain situation. For example Johnson & Johnson's core values led the company to voluntarily remove Tylenol from the market after the cyanide poisoning of some Tylenol capsule users, even though this act cost the company more than $100 million.

The mission also includes the company's core purpose. An effective purpose statement doesnot just describe products or services; it captures people's idealistic motivation for why the organization exists.

The mission of the company serves as the glue that holds the organization together in times of change and guides strategic choices and decisions about the future. All the stakeholders must be allowed to participate in developing a mission statement.

Characteristics of the Effective Mission

- The mission statement must be comprehensive enough so that even a new manager can have a **clear view** of what the firm is trying to achieve just by **reading** the mission statement.
- Each phrase of the mission statement must clarify the firm's **intentions**.
- The top management must **believe** in the statement in its totality and detail.
- The **inspiring purpose** must **avoid** playing to the **selfish interest** of the stakeholders.
- The statement should describe the company's responsibilities to its stakeholders and its overall responsibility towards the society.
- It should provide **strategic positioning** to the company.
- The **core values** of the organization must be linked to the purpose.
- These values should resonate and reinforce organization's strategy.
- It must clarify the common **behaviour standards** of the firm.
- The statement must **portrait** the organizational culture.

Spiritual Mission

To endorse spiritual dimension in organizational leadership repertoire we need to start from the organization's mission. The mission of the organization according to modern concept should define the purpose of the organization that provides scope in terms of its operations in range of products and markets. This is of course very important activity to generate efficiency and effectiveness, but prior to business mission the spiritual mission of the organization must be created.

The spiritual mission should include right intentions and various spiritual values that organization wants to keep and are to be lived by its people. This may be worded in various ways out of which one we are mentioning as hereunder:

"We are involved in generating wealth for the society and contributing graciously in preserving our planet as a sweet home for all living creatures. We are committed to provide our divine services to all humans without any expectations".

The spiritual mission provides an organization the accurate reason for its existence. It can be a strong guiding force behind all the employees to bring them into the mode of graciousness. This can also be an important tool to develop gracious work culture in the organization.

24

Mentorship

Mentorship is a process by which the skills, knowledge, values and life experiences of a selected, successful manager are transmitted to another employee in the organizational system, for the purpose of growing that employee for greater efficiency and effectiveness (Nasser and Vivier 1995).

WHAT IS MENTORING?

Mentoring is cooperative and nurturing relationship between a more experienced person and a less experienced person. It is the best way to clone the corporate knowledge. It helps to develop great leaders who must train future leaders. It helps an employee to reach full personal and professional potential.

Mentoring provides the best way to customize the development of careers to serve corporation's mission and helps in developing corporate culture. Since mentorship develops relationships between leaders and followers hence, it allows employees to share their knowledge and talent. It helps greatly in generating commitment of employees with the organizational values and in developing high performance organizational culture, competencies and core competencies.

Mentor is a person whom you trust to have your best interests at heart, someone who would risk telling you what you need to know even though that it might be painful to you (Missirian 1981). In a mentor's role the transformational leader clearly identifies the potentials that are in dormant state in the employees and the critical areas needing work. He provides personalized training to his employees to develop their potentials to the maximum.

Attributes of a Successful Mentor

- As a mentor you must have belief in the value of mentorship and should have the desire to be a mentor.
- You must possess the ability to develop relationships, motivate others, communicate effectively, encourage and praise others, and counsel your subordinates for career path. You should also be able to identify your subordinates' potential and development needs, set clear goals, take moderate risks, and to give and receive feedback.
- To become a successful mentor you must develop an excellent organizational knowledge, excellent subject knowledge, strong leadership qualities, good interpersonal relations, credibility, and loyalty towards the organization.

Role of a Mentor

Building relationship

Develop trustful relationships with people and develop cooperative environment are the prime requirements of mentorship process. The leader in a mentor role is responsible for same.

Acquiring information

Mentors acquire information to understand weaknesses and problems of employees through asking questions, listening empathically, and observing performances. Normally, employees are reluctant to share their problems and feelings with their superiors because of lack of trust. So developing mutual trust is extremely important to acquire correct information.

Vision, mission, goals and objectives

Mentors as visionary leader provides direction to their employees by setting a vision of the organization or a particular unit. They mutually decide the purpose of life of each employee by detecting employee's personal mission. They also mutually set the goals and objectives for each employee in the organization.

Action plans

Leaders with their followers mutually decide the action plans to achieve goals.

Teaching

In a mentorship process, leaders are also performing their role as a teacher. Through good teaching they provide information to employees about business strategy, vision, mission of the organization, organizational values, desired behaviour and services, products and outputs. They need to assist employees in learning new skills. There are some requirements that have to be fulfilled in order to do the good teaching. These are as follows:

- Effective teaching is as much about passion as it is about reason. Leaders not only motivate their employees to learn, but also teach them how to learn. It is all about caring your followers and having a passion for it.
- Leaders need to consider their employees as consumers of knowledge. Good teaching bridges the gap between theory and practice. As a teacher you need to ensure that your employees not only know the organizational mission and values but they should also live it. Unless they believe and feel the mission, they cannot achieve it.
- As a good teacher, you need to be involved sincerely in listening, questioning, and being responsive. You must appreciate that each employee is different and carries different set of potential. Good teaching is about pushing your employees to excel and at the same time it is about being human, respecting others, and being professional at all times.
- Good teacher is flexible, fluid, experimenting and has the confidence to adjust to changing circumstances. Good teaching is about the creative balance between an authoritarian on the one hand and a softy on the other.
- Effective teaching requires humour. It is often about making innocent and harmless jokes, mostly at your own expense, so that the barriers can be broken and employees learn in a more jubilant and relaxed atmosphere.
- Effective teaching is actually caring, nurturing, and developing minds and talents. It is about devoting time, often invisible, to every employee.
- Effective teaching is supported by strong and visionary leadership. It is continually reinforced by an overarching vision that transcends the entire organization and is reflected in what is done.

Coaching

In the mentorship process, coaching is a very important activity for the development of people and organizations. Coaching is not just the looking for and fixing the weaknesses rather it is about building on a performer's strengths and values. It is also about helping others to realize their noblest visions, values and ideas. Coaching is low cost means of improving an employee's performance in the organization. It entails the supervisor's instructions to subordinates in order to develop subordinates' potential. Proper coaching maximizes the potential of the employee. It improves the learning opportunities for both the supervisor and subordinate, and leads to greater flexibility and adaptability in the workplace. Coaching is built on the foundation of trust.

Identify Hidden Potential and Development Needs

All human beings are carrying tremendous potentials in them, but they are not aware of those. Once Albert Einstein said, "I think I used about 25% of my intellectual capacity during my life." According to William James (1897, republished in 1956), human beings use only 10–12 % of their potential, rest 90% is always in dormant state. The saddest part of most people's lives is that they die with the music still in them. Here you have to perform your role as a coach. You have to dug out the hidden potentials of your employees and help them to develop the same. Through the strength and weakness analysis of employees you identify the areas needing work. Provide effective leadership and counselling for the achievement of goals and objectives.

Coaching Methodology

There should be three basic processes involved in coaching that are diagnosis, counselling and monitoring. Diagnosis is a process whereby a supervisor continuously observes and interprets a subordinate's performance and behaviour. Counselling is a continuous process by which the supervisor provides the necessary advice to subordinates in order to help them improve their performance, and to further develop themselves. Monitoring provides the follow-up process a supervisor applies to determine the extent to which a subordinate's performance is measuring up to set standards.

Spiritual Dimensions in Mentoring

When an employee joins an organization, he is not aware of the organizational values and the required behaviour. In a mentor's role, the transformational leader clearly identifies the potentials that are in dormant state in the employees and the critical areas needing work. He provides personalized training to his employees to develop their potentials to the maximum. He also ensures that employees should raise their belief in organization's values and behave according to organizational culture.

But as a mentor the role of a leader goes much beyond than the presently defined. Because even in a high-performing organizational culture, it has been observed that the employees do not know what satisfies them, why they are greedy, envious, egoist, and anguish through comparisons. Therefore, it is a duty of a leader to preach his subordinates about different modes of material nature (lunacy, obsession, and graciousness) and their consequences. Through mentoring, teaching, coaching, training, and leading by example a leader should get his subordinates into the mode of graciousness, so that everyone can contribute effectively in achieving organization's spiritual mission and can reach to a destination where satisfaction and peace of mind exists.

25

Fostering Teamwork

It is a reality of organizational life that one can rarely be successful alone. Teams outperform individuals acting alone, especially when performance requires multiple skills, judgments and experiences. In business organizations effective teamwork is a mantra for success. In any situation requiring the real-time combination of multiple skills, experiences and judgments, a team without doubt give better results than a collection of individuals operating within confined job roles and responsibilities. Today, the leaders and followers must first learn critical new skills, values, and behaviours, and then work to institutionalize those behaviours to sustain high performance. We believe teams are essential to such objectives because they have always induced behavioural changes. Teams bring together complementary skills that exceed those of any individual on the team. This mix of skills and experiences enable teams to respond to multifaceted challenges like innovation, quality, and customer service.

WHAT IS A TEAM?

"A team is an energetic group of people who are committed to achieve common objectives, who work well together, and enjoy doing so, and who produce quality results." According to Katzembach and Smith (1993), "a team is a small number of people with complementary skills who are committed to a common purpose, performance, goals and approach for which they hold themselves mutually accountable."

A team is a group of people coming together to collaborate. This collaboration is to reach a shared goal or task. A group of people is not necessarily a team. A team is a group of people with a high degree of interdependence geared towards the achievement of a common goal or completion of a task, it is not just a group for administrative convenience. A group, by definition, is a number of individuals having some unifying relationship.

Team members are deeply committed to each other's personal growth and success. That commitment usually transcends the team. A team outperforms a group and outperforms all reasonable expectations given to its individual members. That is, a team has a synergistic effect, one plus one equals a lot more than two.

Team members not only cooperate in all aspects of their tasks and goals, they share in what are traditionally thought of as management functions, such as planning, organizing, setting performance goals, assessing the team's performance, developing their own strategies to manage change, and securing their own resources. A work group becomes a team when leadership becomes a shared activity, accountability shifts from strictly individual to both individual and collective, the group develops its own purpose or mission, problem solving becomes a way of life, not a part time activity, and effectiveness is measured by the group's collective outcomes and products (Table 25.1).

TABLE 25.1 Primary Differences between Groups and Teams

Group	*Team*
• Has a designated, strong leader.	• Leadership roles are shared.
• No consensus on common approach.	• Consensus on common approach is generated consciously.
• Commitment in personal relationship among group members vary and in most of cases within the organizational boundaries.	• Commitment in personal relationship among team members is similar and goes beyond the organizational boundaries.
• Individual responsibility and accountability.	• Mutual responsibility and accountability.
• The group's and organization's missions are alike.	• Team has its explicit mission.
• Group performance is collection of individual performances.	• Team members' performed collectively.
• Hierarchical structure is prominent and individual accountabilities are dissimilar.	• Horizontal structure is prominent individual accountabilities are similar.
• Feedback is given by higher position to lower positions.	• Mutual feedback, open-ended discussion, active problem solving.
• The group may be of large number of people.	• The number of people in the team is essentially small.

A team has following **four** major benefits for the organization:

1. It maximizes the organization's human resources. Each member of the team is coached, helped, and led by all the other members of the team. A success or failure is felt by all members, not just the individual. Failures are not blamed on individual members, which give them the courage to take chances. Successes are felt by every team member, this helps them to set and achieve bigger and better successes. In addition, failure is perceived as a learning lesson.
2. There are superior outputs against all odds. This is due to the synergistic effect of a team, a team can normally outperform a group of individuals.
3. There is continuous improvement. No one knows the job, tasks, and goals better than the individual team members. To get real change, knowledge, skills, and abilities are needed. When they pull together as a team, they will not be afraid to show what they can do. Personal motives will be pushed to the side to allow the team motive to succeed.
4. Existence of "high performance teams" at all levels of the organization transforms an average organization into "high performance organization".

TEAM FUNDAMENTALS

Most teams are simply a collection of individual relationships with boss where everyone is contesting with each other for gaining power and position. These are not teams. A team is small number of people with complementary skills who are committed to a common purpose, performance goals, and approach for which they hold themselves mutually accountable.

From above statement, it is clear that a leader has to continuously work on team fundamentals like appropriate number of people, complementary skills, team members' commitment with team's mission, goals, and with common approach, and individual and mutual accountability. Figure 25.1 represents these important team fundamentals on which you must concentrate to build effective team.

Small Number

The large numbers of people have trouble interacting constructively as a group. Ten people are more likely than fifty to successfully work through their individual, functional and hierarchical differences toward a common plan and hold themselves mutually accountable for the results.

Small number is more pragmatic in order to work productively with common approach, complementary skills, and mutual accountability. The right size of team should be of 2 to 15 members. A larger number of people say, fifty or more can theoretically become a team. But groups of such size more likely will break into sub-teams rather than function as a single team.

Complementary Skills

Common sense tells us that it is a mistake to ignore skills when selecting a team. A team cannot get started without some minimum complement of skills, especially technical and problem solving ones. And no team can achieve its purpose without developing all the skill levels required.

Team should carry right blend of complementary skills, that is, each of the complementary skills are necessary to do the team's job. These skills fall into four categories as follows (Figure 25.1):

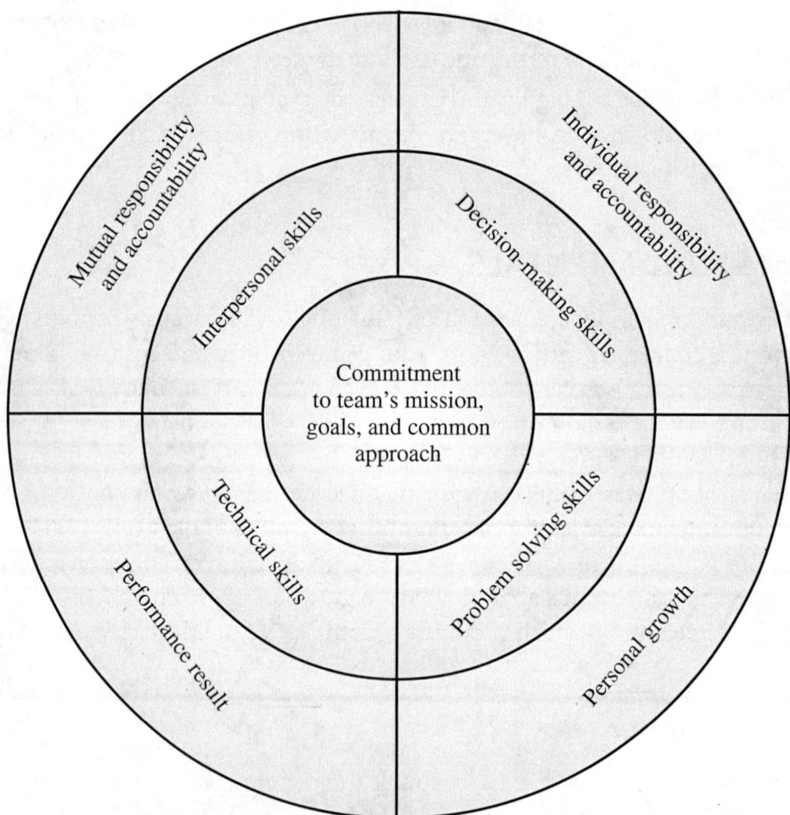

Figure 25.1 Team fundamentals.

Technical skills

In product based organizations, there must be technical experts like marketers, engineers, and IT experts. If a team is having only marketers, then they may not be able to generate excellence where engineering skills and knowledge is required. Thus, to generate excellence and achieve success in the market, we should have right mix of experts of different field so that they can complement each other.

Problem solving skills

Teams must be able to understand the difference between problems and symptoms. In all work settings, the actual problem is beneath the thick layers of symptoms. There should be some experts who can really remove these symptoms and dug out the actual problem. They should possess drill-down problem solving approach to correct the situation from the core.

Decision-making skills

A decision is the result of making a judgment or reaching a conclusion. Decision-maker should possess the skill to determine various alternatives and make rational choice among them. Decision-making is a part of all managers' jobs. A manager is constantly making decisions while performing the functions of planning, organizing, staffing, directing, and controlling. Decision-making is not a separate, isolated function of management but a common core to the other functions.

Interpersonal skills

Common understanding and purpose cannot arise without effective communication and constructive conflict that in turn depend on interpersonal skills. These include risk taking, helpful criticism, objectivity, active listening, giving the benefit of the doubt, support, and recognizing the interests and achievements of others.

Individual Accountability and Personal Growth

Real team is a vehicle for personal learning and development. Team's performance focus helps teams to quickly identify skill gaps and the specific development needs of team members to fill them. Each team member's sense of individual accountability to the team promotes learning. Once harnessed to common purpose and set of goals, natural individualism motivates learning within teams. Except for certain technical and functional skills, most of us have the potential to learn skills needed in teams. The individual accountability drives the majority of us to find some way to make our own distinctive and individual contributions to the team.

Commitment to Team's Mission and Goals

A team's purpose and performance goals go together. The team's short-term performance goals must always contribute to the team's purpose. The best teams invest a tremendous amount of time and effort exploring, shaping, and agreeing on a purpose that belongs to them both collectively and individually. A common meaningful purpose sets the tone and aspiration. Groups that fail to become teams rarely develop a common purpose or team's mission that they own and can translate into specific and actionable goals.

Specific performance goals are an integral part of the purpose. Transforming broad directives into specific and measurable performance goals is the definite first step for teams trying to shape a common purpose meaningful to its members. Specific goals, e.g. "getting a new product to market in less than half the normal time provides clear communications and constructive conflict within the team. The attainability of specific performance goals helps teams maintain their focus on generating results. Challenging goals also motivate team members to add certain meaning to the organization.

Commitment to a Common Approach

It is important to develop common approach to accomplish performance results. Team members must agree on who will do particular jobs, how schedules will be set an adhered to, what skills are to be developed, the conduct of each member to be in a team, and the criteria and style of making and modifying decisions, including when and how to modify its approach to get the job done. Agreeing on the specifics of work and how it fits together to integrate individual skills and development, lies at the heart of generating commitment to a common approach.

Mutual Accountability

No group ever becomes a team until it can hold itself accountable as a team. At its core, team accountability is about the sincere promises we make to ourselves and others for being accountable to the team's goals and performance results. To generate mutual accountability the trust is extremely significant. The members must be proactive in their habit as proactive persons understand their responsibility to take the initiatives to achieve team's mission and goals and consider themselves accountable for consequences.

Performance Results

In the final examination, the performance is both the cause and effect of teams. Without specific, tangible performance results, in fact, little else matters. If you want to know whether any particular group is a real team, look first at its performance results.

To work effectively on team basics and to build real team, as a team leader in actual setting you need to ask some questions to yourself and to find the answers.

The questions are compiled in Table 25.2. Answering these questions can establish the degree to which your group functions as real team, as well as help to pinpoint how you can strengthen your efforts to increase performance. They set high standards, and answering them honestly may reveal a tougher challenge than you have expected. At the same time, facing up to the answers can speed up your progress in achieving the full potential of your team.

TABLE 25.2 Questions to be Asked to Assess Genuineness of Team

1. Does your team have small number of people?
   - Can team members develop mutual relationships with each other and communicate easily?
   - Do you have enough number of people so that you can have sub-teams?
   - Do people know each other's nature, strengths and weaknesses?
2. Do your team members possess all types of required skills needed?
   - Do team members are ready to learn different skills?
3. Are your team members at the consensus for common approach?
   - Is the approach meticulous and understood by each team member?
   - Is it developed mutually?
4. Does your team have well-defined team's mission?
   - Does it contribute to achievement of organizational mission?
   - Does all the members know and believe in the team's mission?
   - Does all the members are committed to team's mission?
   - Do all the members refer to mission before making strategic decisions?
5. Are the team goals clearly defined and contributing to team's mission?
   - Are they clear, simple, and measurable?
   - Are they defined by team members mutually?
6. Do your team members accept mutual responsibility and accountability?
   - Does mutual trust exist in the environment?
   - Do all the members understand their responsibility to take initiatives?
   - Are all the members feel themselves accountable for results?

LEADERS' BEHAVIOUR AND ATTITUDE FOSTERING TEAMWORK

Successful team leaders instinctively know that the goal is team performance results instead of individual achievement, including their own. They act to clarify purpose and goals, build commitment and self-confidence, strengthen the team's collective skills and approach, remove obstacles, and create opportunities for others. The attitude of the leader is the key for high performing team. Team leaders believe that they do not have all the answers, so they do not insist on providing them. They believe they cannot succeed without everyone's contributions, so they avoid any action that might constrain inputs or intimidate anyone on the team. Majority of managers today perceive authority as the ability to command and control subordinates and to make all the tough decisions. This is sometimes called the **'divine right of managers'**. Such managers believe that they have all the answers.

To build a team, it requires a strong drive to enable people across the board to develop the necessary attitudes to work together. All the leaders must possess a typical behaviour and attitude that foster teamwork in an organizational climate. Table 25.3 lists the teamwork enhancing behaviours that are described in following pages:

TABLE 25.3 Leaders' Behaviour and Attitudes that Foster Teamwork

1. The team's mission should be defined mutually.
2. Generate commitment for excellence.
3. Developing the team's norms.
4. Work as a role model to inspire team members.
5. Build consensus for common approach.
6. Encouraging the use of jargon.
7. Encouraging mutual cooperation among team members.
8. Encouraging competition with the other teams.
9. Challenging the teammates with tough but achievable tasks.
10. Celebrate small wins.
11. Emphasize on mutual feedback.
12. Empower team members.

Defining the team's mission

At the beginning, the leaders must ask their team members to participate actively in team's mission development process. The mission of the team should contain specific goal, purpose, and philosophical tone. Team members' commitment with their mission will improve teamwork. This commitment with the mission provides emotional anchorage to team members and helps them to make relevant decisions. The leaders must establish a climate in which team members can freely express their feelings, ideas, and opinions.

Generate commitment for excellence

Simply performing the job for the sake of doing it is not going to produce world-class results. For generating excellence in the performances requires emotional commitment with the team's mission. Therefore, the team leader's foremost job is to emotionally align each member with the mission, goals and common approach of the team. A standard way to build team spirit is to help the team members realize why they should be proud of their accomplishments.

Developing a norm of teamwork

A team norm is a standard of conduct that is shared by team members and guides their behaviour. Leaders shape team's cultural values and norms to define boundaries of acceptable behaviour and provide a frame of reference as to what is right or wrong. To establish teamwork norm some leaders encourage team members to treat each other as if they were customers, thus, encouraging cooperative behaviour and politeness.

Norms may be written or may evolve as unwritten understandings over time. Most newly organizing teams find it effective to start out with an initial set of norms with the understanding that these will need to be reviewed and modified frequently. Some teams decide to review norms at the beginning or end of each meeting. The establishment and adherence to team norms helps build team discipline, trust between team members, and supports a safe environment. Table 25.4 shows some important team norms.

TABLE 25.4 Sample Team Norms or Guidelines

- Treat each other with dignity and respect.
- Transparency: avoid hidden agendas.
- Be genuine with each other about ideas, challenges, and feelings.
- Trust each other. Have confidence that issues discussed will be kept in confidence.
- Team members will practice a consistent commitment to sharing all the information they have. Share the complete information that you have upfront.
- Listen first to understand, and do not be dismissive of the input received.
- Practice being open-minded.
- Do not be defensive with your colleagues.
- Rather than searching for the guilty, give your colleagues the benefit of the doubt; have a clean slate process.
- Support each other—do not throw each other under the bus.
- Avoid territoriality; think instead of the overall good for the company, your employees, and your customers.
- The discussion of issues, ideas, and directions will not become a personal attack or return to haunt you in the future.
- It is okay to not know the right answer, and to admit it. The team can find the answer.
- Problems are presented in a way that promotes mutual discussion and resolution.
- It is safe to be wrong as a manager. Thoughtful decision-making is expected.

(*Contd.*)

TABLE 25.4 Sample Team Norms or Guidelines (*Contd.*)

- Own the whole implementation of the product, not just your little piece; recognize that you are part of something larger than yourself. Be responsible to own the whole picture.
- Practice and experience humility—each of us may not have all the answers.
- If you commit to doing something, do it. Be accountable and responsible to the team.
- It is okay to be the messenger with bad news. You can expect a problem solving approach, not recrimination.
- Promise to come prepared to your meetings and projects so that you demonstrate value and respect for the time and convenience of others.
- Strive to continuously improve and achieve the team's strategic goals. Do not let ineffective relationships and interactions sabotage the team's work.
- Expend the effort to practice all of these norms and to care enough about the team and its work to confront each other, with care, compassion, and purpose, when a team member fails to practise these norms.

Work as role model to inspire team members

As a leader, you set example in front of your team members by being a positive model of team play. Keep informal communication with team members and generate "we" feeling in the environment.

Build consensus for common approach

A common approach to achieve the tasks is extremely important for higher level of performance. Leaders ask their team members to take initiatives and participate in the process of developing common approach. Teach them how to build consensus by group discussion. The common approach gives constant guidelines to team members to generate synergy in the environment.

Encouraging the use of jargon

Jargon is a specialized language that fosters cohesion and commitment and create bond among team members. It also reinforces unique values, and contributes effectively in developing high performance organizational culture. Jargon helps team members to communicate with fewer misunderstandings among them.

Encouraging mutual cooperation among team members

Most of the existing managers do the common mistake of encouraging competition within the team members. They think that they can motivate their team members through inducing certain competitive reward schemes. This inner competition generates one winner and many other losers. How can you compete with the competitors with a team that have many losers? You need to introduce group reward schemes to generate cooperation among the team members. Giving reward for group accomplishments fosters cooperation and reinforces teamwork because people receive rewards for what they have achieved collaboratively. Recognize whole team as a winner. Recognizing the efforts of outstanding performer is also as important as team recognition. The team should present an award to an outstanding performer as outstanding contributor. This will build teamwork.

Encouraging competition with another group

Encourage rivalry with competitors because beating competition makes more sense when the competition is outside your organization. This develops team cohesiveness and team members get charged to win the competition.

Challenging the teammate with tough but achievable tasks

Always update your team members with latest happenings in the external and internal environment. Put new challenges to them so that they can work together to modify the status quo. These new challenges will break the monotony in work environment, motivate people to bring changes in the system and enhance the teamwork.

Celebrate small wins

Once the team is involved in achieving its mission it becomes important to keep momentum in order to sustain the motivated efforts. This momentum can be granted through celebration of small wins in the way. These small wins can be celebrated in the form of tea session, coffee session, team dinner, and small trips to exotic locations.

"Celebrating small wins is fine, declaring the war won can be catastrophic."

Emphasize on mutual feedback

As a leader, you must collect and provide the feedback about team's performance and the areas require improvement. The team should review and rate its performance as a team. It can discuss the areas of improvements and develop mutual strategies to perform better.

Empower team members

Micromanagers do not trust on their employees' abilities and put excessive controls. They keep the decision-making power with them only and try to direct or interfere in their subordinates' day-to-day activities. These controls inhibit team's performance. As a leader you must work as macromanager who trust and empower their employees and allow them to manage their own activities. This enables team members to perform outstandingly as a team.

HIGH PERFORMANCE TEAMS

Like any real team, the high performance teams are also fulfilling all the team fundamentals, viz. small numbers, complementary skills, team's mission and goals, common approach, and mutual accountability described earlier in this chapter. But the high performance teams differentiate themselves from real teams on the basis of degree of commitment, particularly how intensely the team members are committed to each other. Such commitments go much beyond common courtesies and teamwork. The team members' commitment to each other continues beyond even the life of the team itself. This commitment is not just the deep intimacy between team members rather it is everyone's strong personal commitment to one another's development, advancement and success. Energized by this extra sense of interpersonal commitment the team's purpose become more gracious for team members. People start considering one member's failure as their failure. The mutual concern for each other's development and success leads to the development of interchangeable skills among team members and generate greater flexibility in the team. In the high performance teams the leadership role is rotated and shared with much more flexibility than real teams. The team members carry much better sense of contribution, humour and fun.

The Indian cricket team under the captainship of Mr. M.S. Dhoni went to South Africa in 2007 to participate in ICC 20-20 World Cup Cricket Tournament. This team was young and inexperienced, and was rated low in comparison to Australian, South African, and British teams. Like other teams Indian team also had its mission to win the world cup along with other team fundamentals such as complementary skills and mutual accountability. But the Captain of Indian team had some different idea in his mind and that was interpersonal commitment. With his marshalled efforts, the entire Indian team made commitment to support and cheer up each other for best performance in the field. This commitment generated intense emotional bond among team members and a very high energy level. Suddenly, the whole team got rid off the fear of failure and filled with full of humour and fun. They started generating excellence for the sake of performance in the field and got detached from anxiety of winning or losing. This led to some miraculous performances on the field by Indian players which they themselves could not believe and they won the world cup and pride for India.

26

Motivation

Motivated employees are the essence of any organization and the main source of ensuring a sustainable competitive advantage.

WHAT IS MOTIVATION?

Motivation is willingness to exert high level of effort to achieve organizational goals conditioned by efforts and abilities to satisfy some individual needs. It is a set of processes that determine behavioural choices. Motivation is the vital link that exists between knowing and doing, thinking and action, and competence and performance. According to classical need based theories, motivation is a result of the interaction of a person's internalized needs and external influences that determine the behaviour designed to achieve the goal.

As a leader, it is your job to induce this willingness among your employees so that they can put an effort to achieve organizational and personal goals. To induce this willingness among your employees you need to inspire them to motivate themselves. Inspiration is a thought and motivation is an action so you need to induce fruitful thoughts into your subordinates' mind, you have to change their thoughts. When thinking changes it reflects in behaviour.

WHAT MOTIVATE EMPLOYEES?

The earlier understanding of motivation was that it is driven by external factors. Many business organizations still believe that salary increases and bonuses are enough to motivate people. Unknown to them the employee of today needs to be internally motivated to function optimally.

Although the classic approaches given by Maslow (1943), Herzberg (1968), and McClelland (1971) had the right idea to motivate people but it is often ineffective because it focuses on external control and offers external inducements.

Csikszentimihalyi's Concept of "Flow" Experiences

According to Csikszentimihalyi (1990), people experience "flow" when:

- A particular task is enjoyable and possess fun.
- They enjoy a particular challenge.
- They possess the skills required to perform the task.
- They experience a personal sense of freedom and control.

These "flow" experiences motivate people to re-engage in certain activities with even more energy. Csikszentimihalyi's research revealed the following barriers to "flow" in the companies:

- Task lack challenge and variety.
- Tough management controls.
- Overbearing structures and hierarchies.

He observed that there are ample opportunities for "flow", but it seldom happened. The main reason for this is probably that it is very difficult to trust others completely and to let go of control.

The Concept of Self-systems

Self-perception has been found to play an important role in enhancing or limiting motivation. People's behaviour is guided by how they see themselves. People will pursue goals which they feel they can prosecute in order to ensure positive feedback on their competence.

Bandura's Social Cognitive Theory

Bandura's (1986) research created a valuable framework for understanding self-directed behaviour. The following self-systems were identified:

Self-monitoring

People use feedback from others and they task to adjust their behaviour.

Self-evaluation

People compare their performance with their perception of their competence. Their perception about themselves as highly competent person may lead to increased efforts.

Self-efficacy

People's belief that they can cope effectively with a particular situation, in other words belief in their competence. People with high self-efficacy are highly motivated.

Utilizing above research findings you can motivate your people by empowering and encouraging them for self-reinforcement, self-goal setting, self-criticism, self-observation/evaluation, and self-expectation. Maximum performance motivation is obtained when people set goals for themselves at top level of their perceived capability.

Previous beliefs that motivation is influenced only by external factors have therefore, been changed by recent research findings that internal factors, namely emotional choice and/or self-perception, play a prominent role. The concept of motivation has therefore, undergone a shift in emphasis from external to internal. It has been proven that internal motivation is more powerful and lasting in determining the behaviour of individuals than external motivation.

Another major barrier to motivation is the failure of management to perceive what employees really want. A study by Kenneth (1978) revealed that a manager thinks that an employee wants gross salary, job security, promotion, growth, and good working conditions. But in reality, employee wants interesting work, full appreciation of work done, job security, and feeling of belongingness.

> *"The biggest disease today is not leprosy or tuberculosis but rather the feeling of being unwanted."*
>
> Mother Teresa Quotes

The only way to find out what really motivate people is by objective observation. One can learn a lot about a person by looking at the choices he or she makes. This shows you what is important to that person and they can then be motivated accordingly.

HOW TO ENHANCE MOTIVATION?

Following elements are very crucial to ensure motivation and that must be incorporated in the organizational culture:

Allow Employees Full Autonomy and Control

Motivation is at highest when employees are given full control over a specific task. They must, therefore, be given the freedom to decide what has to be done, how it will be done and at what speed. In a nutshell, they should be given room to be creative and innovative. This allows employees to fully identify with their jobs, which is very rewarding and leads to high productivity. This implies that the role of management must change from an authoritarian to a supportive role. The manager must learn to avoid interfering in day-to-day activities. The role changes to:

- being a source of information and experience.
- coordinate and develop strategies for the future.
- be a role model and a coach.
- more the individuals are empowered, more the responsibility they will exhibit.
- a barrier to motivation, when people are given responsibility without empowerment.

Create Learning Opportunities

This allows individuals to acquire new skills and growth. This enables them to meet even more difficult challenges. The process of learning itself is a very rewarding experience. Being able to meet more difficult challenges through requiring new skills is deeply motivating. The best results are achieved when skills and challenges are in balance. Learning refreshes people mentally and culture of continuous learning adds to personal mastery and self-esteem. The more people know, the broader the base is from which they generate ideas and solve problems.

Encourage Teamwork

Being a part of team makes work more enjoyable and stimulating. Team provides supporting environment to an individual. Team members are allowed to choose their own level of challenge and this is not stagnant, but can change depending on the situation at hand. Team members are exposed to diversity which facilitates cross-training in terms of exchanging skills and increased flexibility. This makes work more interesting and enjoyable.

Ensure Positive Work Environment

If you are hearing that there are internal conflicts or office politics that are creating an unpleasant work environment, as a leader you are the one who can fix it. The fact that you listened, and you acted, will be a sign that you care about creating a positive place to work.

Management by Objective

This entails that both managers and employees are involved in setting specific goals mutually to obtain overall organizational objectives and evaluation of progress. It is imperative that unrestricted input from employees is allowed. You might break the discussion into the following areas:

- Performance goals and objectives
- Skills and knowledge development
- Processes and methods
- Feedback, etc.

Participative Management

This encourages increased commitment to the success of the organization. This could include program by which employees can acquire stock in the company as part of their benefits. Another example is the formation of self-managed teams.

Job Enrichment and Redesign

These include the formation of natural work groups to help employees understand their role in the total structure of the organization. Combining tasks to increase variety and make employees feel that meaning has been added to their work might also increase motivation.

Modified Work Schedule

This allows workers to adjust schedules to suit their needs, e.g. working with flexi timing and allowing people to perform some or all of their work away from the standard office settings (so-called virtual offices).

Offer Training Opportunities

Today, employees typically consider employer-sponsored training to be welcomed as a valuable opportunity. They appreciate any workplace training they can receive because it helps to build their skills and also helps to keep them on the job. However, in today's high-tech world, you need to offer a variety of development opportunities, including online learning as well as traditional classroom training and on-the-job skill development. This is particularly true for new generation employees who might be tempted to leave an organization if they are not utilized to their full potential.

Provide On-the-job Coaching

For many years, coaching has been recognized as the critical difference in employees' success. A sincere pat on the back is greatly appreciated by all employees and is an inexpensive and convenient retention tool for most companies. But coaching is about much more than just offering flattery or empty praise. In the role of coach, you are charged with teaching employees and providing them with specific feedback on their performance. Individual attention is a critical component in making employees feel valued, as well as improving their performance. Mentoring is another proven approach to help employees develop the skills and experience necessary to succeed. And nothing motivates better than success!

Provide a Challenging Work

The most credible research on motivation over the past 50 years demonstrates that employees are most motivated by the work itself, and that everything else is secondary. No job necessarily has to be routine, dull or demotivating. There are job redesign strategies available to help renew employees' interest and re-kindle enthusiasm. New tasks, new projects and new responsibilities can help to make your employees' jobs more challenging. If you do not attempt to stretch your people, you may risk losing them.

Cultivate an Atmosphere of Respect

Employees of every generation do not respond well to feeling like just another number, a cog in the wheel, or an invisible part of the organization. All employees need to feel their efforts are recognized and genuinely appreciated. The issue goes beyond being flexible, providing feedback or creating meaningful tasks. Respect your employees' needs, acknowledge their individuality and provide fair opportunities. Make your employees feel valued and they will value their continued employment with the company.

All the strategies are text book issues and can only be successful if employees are given the authority to make choices without an external control. The bottom line is that each section of a company should run like a mini-business and employees should take full control and responsibility. Mutual trust is, therefore, essential.

DEMOTIVATORS

Majority of managers perform many important activities wrongly and create demotivators in the environment. It is very important for you as a leader to ensure that all the activities are followed correctly and all the demotivators are removed from the workplace. The common demotivators are mentioned as hereunder:

Performance evaluation

Performance evaluation can produce demotivation if it is not performed correctly. Few examples of its wrong implementation are as follows:

- Employees are unsure of their role in the work environment if no performance evaluation is done.
- Employees feel that performance evaluation is done only because it has to be done.
- Managers use performance evaluation not as a feedback for employees rather as weapon against them to give them threatening.
- In some instances, it is perceived as a destructive session in which employees are being told how badly they are doing, this is done to avoid rewards and to keep organization's cost low.

Feedback on performance

Inadequate feedback on performance produce demotivation when:

- Employees do not perform because they do not know what good performance is.
- If feedback is not given employees do not know if performance on par – should I improve or not?

Vague instructions

Unclear job descriptions cause people to feel inadequate especially when they do not know what is expected.

No recognition

Team will feel demotivated if no recognition is given for a job well done. Sincere recognition encourages employees.

Recognition given where it was not earned

Recognition is given to the wrong person create demotivation to other employees.

No sense of achievement

If your recommendations are not implemented. Individuals do the least and still get promoted.

Role overload

Too much work in insufficient time produce poor quality of work and demotivation.

Poor planning

Poor planning leads to wastage of time, poor performance, and demotivation.

Incompetence

Employees that do not have knowledge to use equipment and are not willing to learn get demotivated.

Development

If no opportunity exists to be creative and innovative within workplace and employees are not able to develop their full potential, demotivation takes place.

Poor and tense work environment

Following are the symptoms of poor and tense work environment that create demotivation:

- Colleagues that have personal differences, engage in destructive criticism, possess disloyalty among them, do gossip, and are unfriendly.
- Too much rationalization for poor performance.
- Employees do not know about organization's vision and mission.
- Lack of leadership.
- Unchallenging and uninteresting tasks.
- Unfair leave system.
- Lack of team work, and no team goals.
- No empowerment.

Bureaucracy

Following are some features that create demotivation among workers.

- Too many rules, regulations and excessive procedures.
- Over supervision.
- Lack of accountability.
- Delayed implementation of proposals.

A REFRESHING APPROACH TO MOTIVATION

When companies want to change the purchasing behaviour of their customers they rely on advertising agencies 'expertise in persuasion', but when they want to change the behaviour of their own employees in a certain direction, they call it motivation. (Hershey 1993).

Hershey believes that employees can be persuaded to do a specific task by their managers, but this differs from motivation. Motivation can follow on persuasion when the employee finds the persuaded behaviour desirable and is subsequently motivated to repeat it. Employers should, therefore, concentrate on understanding the psychology of advertising, rather than theories of motivation. Effective communication is essential to the art of persuasion. Robert Hershey, therefore, believes that persuasion techniques used by marketing departments can be useful motivational tools. The following approaches should be considered:

- Opinions by experts are persuasive. Important people or big names can make your argument seem more convincing.
- Testimonials of trustworthy and credible employees who are similar to the target audience are more believable.
- Logos—repetition of the message increases the amount of times the target audience thinks about the message.
- Independent multiple sources that support the same message have been shown to be effective.
- Examples or case histories are more potent persuaders than statistics.
- Pathos—getting people to feel happy, sad, or angry can help your argument.
- Ethos—if people believe and have trust in you, you are more likely to persuade them.

Hershey offers a refreshing viewpoint and it might be worthwhile for companies to consider using the same persuasion tools used for advertising to promote desirable behaviour in employees. If employees can be motivated by this way, motivation might be a lot easier because persuasion can generate people's belief. People will do lot for money, more for good leader, but do the most for their belief. People die for their belief. Hershey's viewpoint definitely has merits and should be investigated further.

SPIRITUAL DIMENSIONS IN MOTIVATION

According to Maslow's need hierarchy theory (1943) satisfying lower order needs (food, clothing, shelter, and security) of workers are key factors in motivation and once the lower order needs get satisfied the workers move towards the higher order need categories, e.g. self-esteem and self-actualization needs. But more often than not, it does not happen like that. It is observed quite frequently that high salaried people with higher status try to generate their strengths and satisfaction from their possessions (money, property, gold, and car). They are highly scared of losing their possessions. On the contrary, a lowly paid school teacher, a self-employed artisan, or a priest may well demonstrate a higher level of self-actualization despite poorer satisfaction of their lower-order needs.

This situation can be explained by theory of "self-transcendence" promulgated in Bhagavad Gita (Prabhupada 2003). According to this theory, a person who reaches the mode of graciousness and surrenders his greed, envy, egotism, and status to the feet of Lord Krishna, and embraces sense of contribution and integrity, becomes transcendent. A person in self-transcendence stage is free from endless needs and desires and knows that the meaning of his existence is not to fulfill his needs and desires rather to give divine service to society by gaining and disseminating knowledge and generating excellence in his work. Self-transcendent person sacrifice his lower-order needs for higher goals and achieve satisfaction and peace of mind through a sense of contribution and service. Therefore, the motivation comes from 'sacrificing rather than satisfying', or through 'charity rather than acquisitions'.

This "sense of service" and "sense of contribution" has another impact on amplitude and sustainability of happiness, satisfaction, and peace of mind. Imagine that you are living at an island alone and receive appreciation letter from the head of the country for your good work done, you may not feel happy for more than few seconds as there is no one to share your success and the amplitude of you happiness and satisfaction will be negligible. Now, imagine you are working in a company and for your better performance you are recognized and get promotion and salary hike, you can be happy and satisfied for a day or so by sharing your achievement with your colleagues, friends and family members, they all will congratulate you for once but then your achievement would become past event and also the amplitude of your happiness and satisfaction will be just medium and fading. Now, consider you are working within a team and your entire team gets success. In this case, all the team members will share the success and happy moments with each other several times and your sense of happiness will be sustained for long time with higher amplitude and it will always motivate you. Therefore, the group success is more important than individual success. Consider with a sense of contribution and service if your team is doing something meaningful for the society then the whole society or country will share your team's success and the amplitude of your happiness and satisfaction would be the maximum and unfading. The sustainability of happiness, satisfaction and peace of mind would also be long lasting. Therefore, it looks imperative that as a true leader we should induce this "sense of contribution and service" to our subordinates or into our organizational culture for long lasting happiness, satisfaction, peace of mind, and to attain the state of self-transcendence and organizational-transcendence.

27

Empowerment

Empowerment is the process of increasing the capacity of individuals or groups to make choices and to transform those choices into desired actions and outcomes. Empowerment broadly can be defined as giving employees the power to do their jobs and make choices and decisions. To empower your employees you need to trust them and be ready to tolerate their imperfections. Empowered people are more involved in the work, take on difficult task and act confidently. They put more sincere efforts to complete the task efficiently and effectively.

The most common understanding of managers about empowerment is simply to delegate authority to make choices and decisions or in other words sharing of power with front line employees. But this understanding is not enough for true empowerment and to really design effective empowerment programme you need to understand what must be shared with your employees. Bowen and Lawler (1995) defined empowerment as sharing four important organizational ingredients with front line employees. These are: information about the organizational performance standards; knowledge that enables employees to contribute effectively in organizational performance; rewards based on the organization's performance; and last but not the least the power to make decisions that influence organizational direction and performance. Bowen and Lawler further added that if any one of four ingredients is missing then the empowerment would be zero.

Spreitzer (1995) mentioned about psychological empowerment, which is actually a motivational construct and have four elements. These four elements of motivational construct are: meaning—adherence to mission; development of competencies; self-determination to achieve performance standards of the organization; and positive impact of empowerment on performance.

Combining the Bowen and Lawler's ingredients and Spreitzer's elements of psychological constructs you can get proper understanding of empowerment. It suggests that empowerment is a process whereby a culture of empowerment is developed. In the culture of empowerment, you need to concentrate on the following key areas:

Confidence

Ensure that your employees possess necessary skills and knowledge to do the job. Also make sure the availability of resources that are needed to perform the job effectively. Demonstrate that you value them and have confidence in their capability and sincerity. Your facial expression, body language, and expressed words must communicate what you think about your people.

Clear expectations

Set clear expectations so the employee knows exactly what management expects.

Communication

Share information with employees in the form of shared vision, mission, goals, and organizational values to provide the common direction, focus and desired behaviour. Also in the form of policies and procedures to set the boundaries for decision-making, performance standards, expected results, and right approaches to perform optimally.

Commitment and support

Support in the form of mentoring and high performance organizational culture to produce the desired results. Provide training and share experiences to develop employees' competencies. Encourage them to develop risk-taking behaviour and innovativeness. Give the feedback to improve upon gray areas. Share power with your people to make their decisions.

Guidance

You must guide your people through listening and asking questions not by simply telling them what to do. People generally know the right answers if they have the opportunity to produce them. When an employee brings you a problem to solve, ask, "What do you think you should do to solve this problem?" Or, ask, "What actions do you recommend?" Employees can demonstrate what they know and grow in the process.

Feeling of being rewarded and recognized

When employees feel under-compensated, under-titled for the responsibilities they take on, under-noticed, under-praised, and under-appreciated; do not expect results from employee empowerment. The employees must possess the feeling of being rewarded and recognized to give you their discretionary energy, that extra effort that people voluntarily invest in work.

Accountability

You hold the employee accountable. If the target is not met or work is not satisfactory, he or she is responsible. You are there for advice, perspective, and guidance, but the employee manages the solution. You do not step in and clean it up. If he is accountable for the solution process, he learns from the problem or error.

Thus, empowerment is defined as, "the process that provides greater autonomy to employees through the sharing of relevant information in the provision of control over factors affecting job performance. This allows employees to have more control and sense of responsibility over their work. Your role as manager shifts from control to facilitation and coordination of work processes. There is less focus on decision-making and more focus on good communications, education and training, and leadership. One of your primary roles becomes to help team members develop their confidence and skills to make good decisions and to maximize their full potential. As a leader your goal is to create a work environment in which people are empowered, productive, contributing, and happy. Trust them to do the right thing. Get out of their way and watch them catch fire. Inspire them to take the action and ensure them that you will be with them and take the responsibility on your shoulders if the consequences are not up to the management's expectations. Whether you have one, ten, or hundred people working for you, you need to make them feel that their actions count.

ADVANTAGES OF EMPOWERMENT

Empowerment provides strong motivation because it meets the higher needs of individuals. Research indicates that individuals have need for self-efficacy, which is the capacity to produce results or outcomes, to feel they are effective. Most people come into organization with the desire to do good job, and empowerment enables leaders to release the already existing motivation among them. The employee reward is intrinsic—a sense of personal mastery and competence.

Empowerment increases the total amount of power in an organization. Simply put, if everyone in the organization has power, then organization is more powerful. The freedom from over-control allows subordinates to utilize their talents and abilities in ways that were otherwise constrained. Empowered employees use more of themselves to do their jobs.

The leaders can devote more time for strategic issues as the empowered employees are able to handle day-to-day problems. Empowered subordinates are able to respond quicker and better to the markets they serve.

WHY EMPLOYEE EMPOWERMENT FAILS?

Lack of belief

Managers often pay lip service to employee empowerment, but do not really believe in its power. They use this term because it is business buzz word. Half-hearted or unbelievable employee empowerment will fail.

Lack of understanding

Most of the managers do not understand the real meaning of empowerment. They delegate the power to their people to take actions but forget other ingredients of empowerment.

Establishing empowerment boundaries

Managers fail to establish boundaries for employee empowerment as in their absence, what decisions can be made by staff members? What decisions can employees make day-by-day that they do not need to have permission or oversight to make? These boundaries must be defined otherwise employee empowerment efforts would be failed.

Micromanagement

Managers defined the decision-making authority and boundaries with staff, but then they micromanage the work of employees. This is usually because they do not trust staff to make good decisions. One HR manager added ten days to the company hiring process because he required his signature at certain milestones in the process. The paperwork was buried on his desk for days, but staff did not proceed without his signature. His lack of trust made employee empowerment a joke. Do employees make mistakes? Certainly, but fooling them about their boundaries is worse.

Decision retrieval

You can help staff to make good decisions by coaching, training, and providing necessary information. You can even model good decision-making, but do not change the empowerment decision unless a serious complication takes place. Teach the employee to make a better decision next time. But do not undermine their faith in their personal competence and in your trust, support, and approbation.

Lack of information-sharing and training

If you fail to provide the information and access to information, training, and learning opportunities needed for employees to make good decisions, do not complain when employee empowerment efforts fall short. The organization has the responsibility to create a work environment that helps foster the ability and desire of employees to act in empowered ways. Information is the key to successful employee empowerment.

Unwillingness to take responsibility

When reporting staff are blamed or punished for failures, mistakes, and less than optimum results, your employees will flee from employee empowerment. If you fail to publicly support decisions and stand behind your employees, it will make them feel deserted.

Absence of rewards and recognition

When employees feel under-compensated, under-titled for the responsibilities they take on, under-noticed, under-praised, and under-appreciated, do not expect results from employee empowerment.

Empowerment helps to remove the conditions that cause powerlessness while enhancing employee feelings of self-efficacy. It also authorizes employees to cope with situations and enables them to take control of problems as they arise. Six broad approaches to empowerment are:

1. Emotional alignment of employees with organizational vision, mission, goals, values, and clarity in mutual expectations.
2. Helping employees achieve job mastery, it means giving proper training, coaching, and guided experience that will result in initial successes.
3. Allowing more control, i.e., giving them discretion over job performance and then holding them accountable for outcomes.
4. Providing successful role models or allowing them to observe peers who already perform successfully on-the-job.
5. Using social reinforcement in persuasion, giving praise, encouragement, and verbal feedback designed to raise self-confidence.
6. Giving emotional support, providing reduction of stress and anxiety through better role definition, task assistance, and honest caring.

When managers use these approaches, employees begin believing that they are competent and valued, their jobs have meaning and impact, and they have opportunities to use their talents. In effect, when they have been legitimately empowered, it is more likely that their efforts will pay off in both personal satisfaction and the kind of results that the organization values.

28

Leading Change

If you think that the way you have worked in the past and got success is the best way to work forever, you are actually stopping the organization from growth. You are where you are because of decisions you took, or did not take sometime in the past. The shape of tomorrow depends entirely on how you act right now. Future is a matter of choice, not chance. If you want to succeed, you should find and strike out on new paths rather than follow the spoilt corridor of accepted success.

WHY CHANGE?

Keeping your organization standstill is the fastest way of moving backwards in a rapidly changing world. According to one saying "there are many who think they understand the situation but what they do not understand is that the situation has just changed". In this speedily changing environment, those who cannot see reason to change, do not want to adjust to change, or unable to change belongs to lost generation.

Today the whole world is changing at rapid pace because of globalization, rapid technological development, increased competition, and changing markets and consumers' attitude. These driving forces are creating threats for those who are not ready to change, and opportunities for those who are implementing changes in their organization.

Complacency, resistance to change and eventual downfall of the organization can easily occur if you do not drive organizational change right through your organization. Organizations that are resistant to change are actually enlarging the gap between their position and the direction in which environmental changes are moving. In fact, as the time goes these change resistant organizations investing major amount of their energy in denying the need for changes and keep them stagnant and alive. The Figure 28.1 shows clearly that these organizations will reach to a point where they will have two choices either to implement radical changes in their systems or die their natural death. But again these radical changes may require greater amount of energy and will face tremendous resistance of employees that may lead to catastrophic event, which can force them to die or lose their business to competitors.

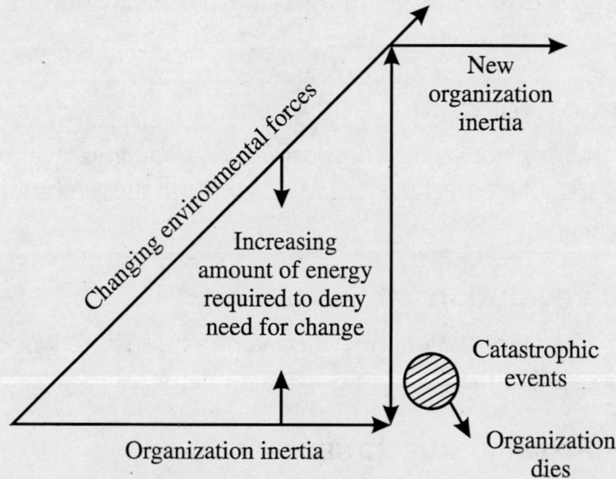

Figure 28.1 The change-resistant organization.

In contrast the change sensitive organizations keep the pace with environmental changes as shown in Figure 28.2. They implement incremental changes as and when they receive warning signals indicating the need to change. In this way the change sensitive organizations are moving in the same direction with the environment, by implementing the needed changes at regular intervals. They require little amount of energy to cope with environmental changes.

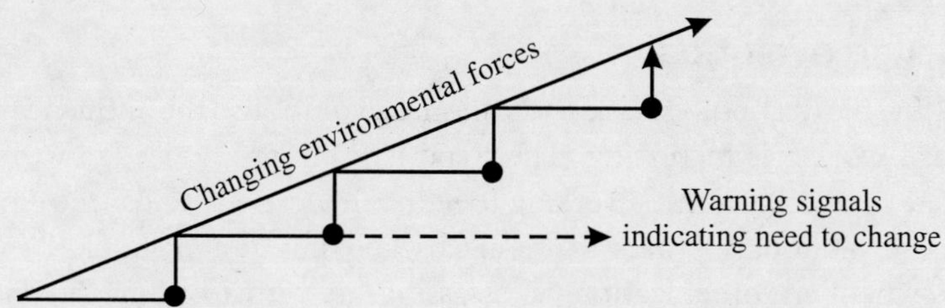

Figure 28.2 The change-sensitive organization.

DRIVING FORCES OF ORGANIZATIONAL CHANGE

The new realities of strategic alliances, telecommuting and global networks have changed the environment in which businesses function. New competitors, playing by different (if any) rules, bring new meaning to the rule of "survival of the fittest". Organizations are under pressure to reduce costs, improve product and service quality, locate new opportunities for growth and increase productivity. Change has become the rule for those organizations seeking corporate survival and success.

There are six distinct but linked evolutions that impact on the nature of business, the structure of organizations and the behaviour and attitudes of managers and workers. These include:

Demographic evolution

Changes are taking place in the composition of populations across the world, which are anticipated to affect the nature of work and the migration of industries across continents.

Competitive evolution

The evolution of the global economy where competition is no longer restricted to national boundaries, rather have gone international.

Evolution of rising expectations

Intelligent and ambitious workers and managers are demanding a greater say over their business destinies and quality of life.

Technology evolution

The pace of technological change is ever increasing.

Educational evolution

The technological evolution and increasing complexity of work processes demand an increasingly skilled and thinking workforce.

Knowledge evolution

Enabled by the technology and educational evolutions, the influence of the knowledge worker is increasing. The trend is now for knowledge workers to collaborate in teams, at times working together in locations across the globe.

These evolutionary processes are inextricably linked and should be viewed as such when an organization is assessing its situation in the business environment.

WHAT TO CHANGE?

Most of the managers know the importance of change, but have poor understanding on what to change or which are the areas in the organization, needed change. Figure 28.3 clearly shows that there are three major thrust areas that need introspection on regular basis.

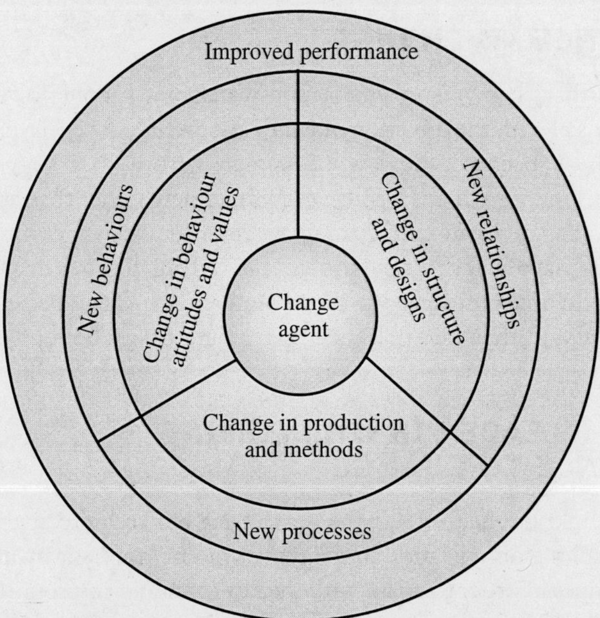

Figure 28.3 Major thrust areas of change.

The first one is the process. The process followed in Production, HR, Finance and Marketing functions. According to changing consumer needs, product preference, buying pattern, markets, lifestyles of people, government policies, and advancement in technology the different processes need to be adjusted in order to satisfy customers with greater value and lower price or premium products, easy accessibility, and better services, etc. The new processes should be invented on regular basis to win the competition on above described dimensions. The structure of the organization the reporting relationships is another important area that need to be adjusted time to time to cope with changing requirements.

The new structures and reporting relationships within the organization helps organizations to avoid complacency in the environment and to increase productivity. These structural changes require cost-benefit analysis, introspection of authority and responsibility attached to every position, and span of control needed to maintain effective controls. Cultural analysis and changes are required to generate competencies and core competencies in the organization.

The behaviour and attitude of the employees are also needed to be improved. The new behaviour and attitude helps people to improve in the way they do things in the organization, in the way they behave internally and externally, values they believe and share, and their commitment with common direction and the purpose of the organization.

RESISTANCE TO CHANGE

We all know that change is inevitable and we cannot survive for long without adjusting our sail with the direction of wind, but even than people naturally resist change. This is because the law of human nature that suggests "people automatically look for what is wrong in anything new rather than what is right". People resist change because they are unaware of future dangers and benefits of change. They have a fear of unknown and are unable to deal with future uncertainty, and are complacent in their comfort zone. They perceive change as personal threat and are afraid that their own kingdom will be toppled.

ROLE OF A LEADER IN OVERCOMING RESISTANCE TO CHANGE

Anyone can hold the helm while the sea is calm but real effective leadership is required to sail the organization in the turbulent environment by implementing required changes in order to adapt with the fast changing environment. Effective leadership during change is a fine balance between envisioning, empowering and energizing. Leaders should concentrate on following stages to successfully overcome people's resistance to change and to involve them with the change process.

Use change vision as a tool to align people

Individuals will be reluctant to involve in change, preferring to cling to the known, if they do not sense the urgent need for change. Change cannot be commanded; rather it requires personal commitment from all involved. People need to be persuaded that change is necessary, and must perceive the change process as inspired by vision and driven by solid corporate values. With this vision, leaders create a sense of hope for the future. As a leader, your first role is to align the diverse workforce with the common direction and provide the sense of destiny or smell of future success.

Utilize empathic communication

As a leader you need to consider the consequences of change for individuals, be aware of how they will be affected and anticipate their reactions. To reduce employees' resistance, you need to display empathy with their experiences and concerns, and communicate effectively about the benefits of change.

Develop credibility

Leaders ignite change by serving as visible role models of the process. They need to create a sense of trust and confidence in their followers. Leading change is about changing oneself (discarding past practices) and communicating values by setting an example with clarity and consistency. Therefore, they must be prepared to change themselves before expecting employees to commit to the change process by changing their own perceptions, attitudes and behaviour. Leaders build trust through success, expertise, personal risk-taking, self-sacrifice and unconventional behaviour. Displaying continuous enthusiasm and support for the project is vital.

THE CHANGE PROCESS

To bring changes successfully in the organization the eight-stage change process, based on the writings of Kotter (1996) and Hambrick, Nadler and Tushman (1997) is given here:

Establishing a sense of urgency

Change leaders need to identify the challenges faced by their organizations by detecting deficiencies, pointing out the sources of distress and clearly presenting the negative consequences of failure to act. They must sense the need for change before competitors do. The organization needs to review its environment (competitors and market forces) in order to assess the current situation and establish potential threats and market opportunities. It is important for the organization to assess the environment as a whole in order to establish the changes that need to be made, and not to focus on a single change factor. Force field analysis suggests the need to identify the forces operating for and against change. To move ahead requires increasing the levels that promote change and reducing the effect of resistors to change. In considering the current situation, it is necessary to evaluate what the consequences of not changing will be. The advantages of change must outweigh the advantages of maintaining the status quo. Besides the importance thereof for the future existence of the organization, this in-depth evaluation is also necessary to enable top-management to gain the support of the people in the organization by reducing complacency with the current situation. People need to be made aware of the costs, also to themselves, of not changing.

Creating the guiding coalition

One individual alone cannot guide a major change effort. A team of representative members is needed, with the right composition, level of trust and shared objective. Four key characteristics of the team include power of position, expertise, credibility and leadership. Leaders need to build coalitions with key power-holders in the organization to spread commitment and cooperation. Teams must be formed which consist of knowledgeable, credible individuals who represent all levels of the organization to drive the change process and ensure that set goals are achieved.

Developing a vision and strategy

Leaders must present viable alternatives to the current situation in the shape of a crystal clear vision, showing why it is the most attractive alternative, and followers need to perceive the change program as realistic. A clear vision clarifies the direction of change, motivates people to take action and helps to coordinate the actions of various people. An effective vision needs to be imaginative, desirable, feasible, focused, flexible and communicable. In this way, it is possible to communicate clearly to the people of the organization what the current situation is and what the potential benefits of the change initiative can be. It can also make it easier for individuals to overcome their fear and resistance to change. Providing a dynamic, clear focus is a powerful mechanism for change and continuous improvement. Focus that cannot be expressed in a simple manner is less likely to be successful. Furthermore, providing continuity in the process is important, as people tend to get nervous when they have nothing to hold on.

Communicating the change vision

Effective communication of the vision is essential to manage fears that employees may have and to gain support for the change process. Effectively communicating the vision to the employees allows them to understand what they are doing, and why. Leaders must be honest and straightforward in the communication, inspiring the employees and providing the motivation to follow the vision. Even if the guiding coalition does not have all the answers, it is important for them to be open and honest. Withholding, or appearing to withhold, important information can create an atmosphere of mistrust among employees. This, in turn, will increase the resistance to change. Various platforms can be used to communicate the changed vision including presentations, internal media, internal broadcasting channels, call centres, posters, informal meetings and memos. Two-way communication is more powerful and preferable over one-way communication. The communication should be kept simple, avoiding technical jargons. Communication must be consistent and the behaviour of senior members of the organization must support the vision.

Empowering broad-based action

Empowerment is the process of giving employees the responsibility, authority and resources to act on their own initiative. Major internal transformation is dependent on the assistance of the employees. However, often these employees feel powerless to help due to limiting or inhibiting factors. These can include formal structures, the lack of necessary skills, personnel, information systems making it difficult to act, and bosses that discourage actions aimed at implementing a new vision. The operating environment of the organization needs to be aligned to the vision of the change imperative. In addition to this, a plan for the development of current employees and, if needed, the recruitment of new employees should be formulated to ensure that the people have the necessary skills and talents required to execute the new strategies.

Generating short-term wins

A short-term win is the celebration of set goals achieved during the process of change and is visible, unambiguous and clearly related to the change effort. In smaller companies, the first short-term wins are often needed within six month's, whereas the larger organizations tend to look at an eighteen-month period. Short-term wins offer the following advantages:

- They reinforce the change effort by showing that the sacrifices made have been worth it.
- Positive feedback builds morale and can increase motivation.
- These wins can assist the guiding coalition in fine-tuning the change vision and strategies.
- Resistance to the change effort is reduced.
- Visible results help to gain/retain the support of management.
- Short-term wins help to build momentum for the change effort.

Consolidating gains and producing more change

Organizations should beware not to allow the sense of urgency for change to decrease when celebrating short-term wins. It is at this vital stage that an organization can regress back to former practices. Major change, especially in larger organizations, can take many years. Factors, which can hinder the full implementation of change, include a turnover of key change agents, exhaustion and bad luck. Ideally, this stage in the change process is characterized by:

- More change, where the guiding coalition uses the credibility created by the short-term wins to attempt bigger change projects.
- More people are brought in and developed to assist with the change process.
- Senior management fulfils the leadership role and keep the level of urgency high.

- Employees from the lower ranks in the organization provide leadership and management for certain projects.
- Unnecessary interdependencies between departments are identified and eliminated, making change easier.

Insert new approaches in the culture of the organization

This is the final step in the transformation process and is dependent on the success and superiority of new over old approaches. Often it is necessary to change the key people in an organization in order to change the culture, as these individuals often personify the old culture. The "paradox of success" states that today's success is tomorrow's status quo. Transformational leaders need to establish a culture of continuous change in their organizations. An organizational culture should be cultivated in a way that encourages people to challenge the established ways of doing things.

29

Shaping Organizational Culture

Basically organizational culture is a personality of any organization. Culture may be broadly defined to include all of the beliefs, values, attitude, rituals and behaviour patterns that people in the organization share. A collective paradigm, which creates relatively homogeneous approach to the interpretation of complexity faces by the organization.

Organizational culture is a pattern of basic assumptions that the group learned as it solved its problems of external adaptation and internal integration that has worked well enough to be considered valid and, therefore, to be taught to new members as the correct way to perceive, think, and feel in relation to those problems (Schein 1990).

Employees are much more likely to want to work for companies that they feel proud of, and where they feel they enjoy a distinctive work environment.

Organizational culture can be thought of as consisting two levels, as illustrated in Figure 29.1. At the core are the invisible psychological objects like expressed values, beliefs and attitudes, which are not visible but can be determined from how people explain and justify what they do. Initially, members of the organization hold these values at a conscious level. For example, at TATA all the employees consciously know that innovation is highly valued and rewarded in the company's culture. But overtime it goes to employees unconscious level and become less open to question, organization's members take them for granted and often it becomes the patterns of social interaction. These assumptions might include:

- Employees are the source of all innovation.

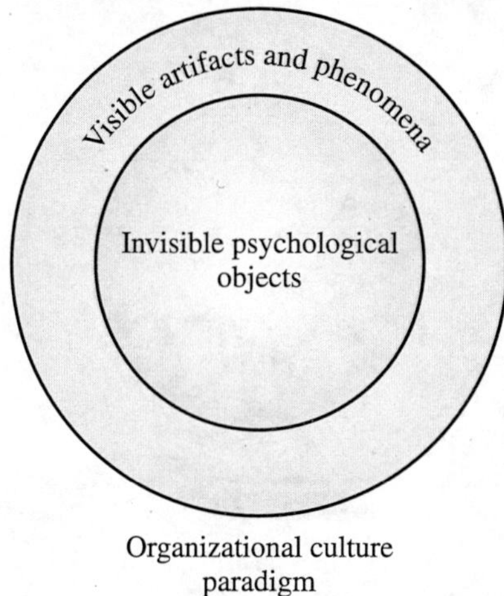

Figure 29.1 Paradigm of organizational culture.

- Organization members are part of a family and will take care of and support each other in taking risks.
- Customer is always right.
- Uncompromised personalized services, and so on.

At the surface level, visible artifacts and phenomena prevails that are actually the reflections of underlying invisible psychological objects through dress style, behaviour patterns, physical symbols, organizational ceremonies, and office layout, etc. At surface level everything one can see, hear, and observe by watching members of the organization. Actually, the way the employees behave depends on their values and belief. Normally, all the people learn behaviour from their own culture, social systems, and family background, but when they work in an organization gradually they start learning behaviour from organizational environment and start believing on organizational values. That is why, an average person performs better in good culture and excellent person perform average in poor culture.

SIGNIFICANCE OF ORGANIZATIONAL CULTURE

In past 25 years, the concept of organizational culture has gained wide acceptance as way to understand human systems. Increased competition in the era of globalization has created greater need for organizational culture. Culture of an organization influences the behaviour of all employees, it guides their decision-making and governs the fundamental manner in which they go about their business. It is hidden, but unifying force that provides meaning and direction to the organization. It is learnt, shared and transferred from employee to employee over time. It emerges naturally from people and systems. Organizational culture is possibly the most critical factor determining an organization's capacity, effectiveness, and longevity. It also contributes significantly to organization's brand image and brand promise. Culture serves three important functions in the organizations:

1. It generates psychological energy needed to generate excellence.
2. Integrates members so that they know how to relate to one another.
3. Helps the organization to adapt the external environment.

Internal Integration

It is culture that guides day-to-day working relationships and determines how people communicate in the organization, what behaviour is acceptable, and how power and status are allocated. Culture can imprint a set of unwritten rules inside employees' minds, which can be very powerful in determining behaviour, thus, affecting organizational performance (Morgan 1993). Culture binds employees together, making the organization a community rather than just a collection of isolated individuals.

External Adaptation

Culture also determines how the organization meets goals and deals with outsiders. The right cultural values can help the organization to respond effectively to customers' needs. Culture can encourage employees' commitment to mission and goals of the organization.

Organizational culture creates energy and momentum. The energy will permeate the organization and create new momentum for success. A high performance organizational culture can help employees to achieve excellence in the way they do things together in internal and external environment. It can convert available organizational resources into certain competences and core competences. The organizational resources can be easily imitated by the competitor, but the competences are extremely difficult to imitate.

CULTURE FOR EXCELLENCE

Today all the organizations are altruistic to develop culture to excel in business. There are basically four driving forces to shape culture that can generate excellence. These driving forces are flexibility, output, coherence, and people.

Flexibility

Flexible organizations are not rigid and willing to change, and to accept and harness opportunities that are present in the environment. They believe to create changes rather than wait for new ideas to come. They do not adopt "best practices" rather create them. The organizations encourage their employees to come with innovative ideas and make them feel that they are the source of innovation. Flexible organizations are actually the learning organizations who want to adapt and implement new processes, technologies and techniques faster than their competitors.

Output

To be a force in a market, as organization must be seen to lead with its products or services. Too much time spent on planning, designing and testing of products and services can reduce organization having to follow. The organization should always achieve first mover advantage and should avoid paralysis by analysis. In 21st century, the market will be merciless with the organizations of me-too strategies.

Coherence

Ensure internal processes of the organization are well established with strong emphasis on adaptability. Energy of people must constantly be aligned to ensure that the output supports the core strategy of the organization.

People

People must be motivated and committed to the organizational norms, values, purposes and goals. This is the most important aspect to ensure success there requires most energy. The emphasis should be given to, ethics, mutual respect, continuous learning and development.

CHARACTERISTICS OF LOW PERFORMANCE CULTURE

It is important to know about low performance culture in order to appreciate high performance organizational culture. Following are the attributes of low performing culture:

- Managers tend to be arrogant, behaving as if they have all the answers and rarely looking outside the firm for new and better business ideas.
- Managers tend to value themselves, their own immediate work groups, and their own particular products and services more highly than anything else.
- These organizations tend to be highly bureaucratic, focusing excessively on procedures, stability, and order.
- Organizational structures are rigid and highly hierarchical.
- People are complacent and do not bother about changing environment.
- People are not committed to organizational mission.

- Internal competition between and even within the departments is given preference in place of cooperation.
- People have very poor relationships with each other and stab each other at the back.
- Compliance is given preference over commitment.
- Punishment and rigid control systems are thought to be the best ways of enhancing employees' performance.
- Managers are reluctant to change and believe in status quo.

Table 29.1 shows the difference between the activities and beliefs of low and high performance culture.

TABLE 29.1 Difference Between Low and High Performance Culture

Low Performance Culture	*High Performance Culture*
Management believes that money is the chief motivator of staff	Management knows that money motivates people to come to work. It does not motivate the way they work
Management does not share information (financial and non-financial) with staff	Management shares information with the staff and asks staff to contribute to this pool of information
All the employees are rewarded on same level regardless of their performance	Managers link employee pay with performance. They have structures in place to measure performance. Staffs are appraised regularly and fairly
Management instructs staff on what to do. Lengthy procedure manuals are produced	Staffs have a set of values that guide them to achieve corporate goals. Personal values and company values coincide (e.g. honesty, integrity, efficiency and care)
Management makes decisions on their own, and tells the staff to follow them	Management asks staff to come up with new ideas, and then encourages them to implement them. The emphasis is given to make the organization transparent
The company is departmentalized, e.g. Marketing Department focuses on the customer and the Human Resources Department focuses on the employee	Employees are grouped in teams that transcend departmental boundaries or able to appreciate the importance of other departments
Employees are viewed as an expense to the company	Employees are viewed as assets and contributors to the company
The company makes a lot of effort to market itself to the outside world. The company does not focus on internal marketing	The company puts a lot of effort into marketing itself to its employees. It keeps employees informed of external marketing objectives

Low performing cultures are number driven organizations. Through lip service, they fool themselves into believing that they are people oriented companies. These organizations preach the importance of team work but their teams are just a group of people that lack members' commitment to team's mission and goals, there is no common accepted approach and possess lack of mutual accountability.

Whereas the high performing cultures are people oriented organizations. They implement specific programmes to make sure the values they have written on paper or organization's wall, are put into action.

ORGANIZATIONAL ENVIRONMENTS

In order to understand low and high performing cultures, you need to first concentrate on three basic dimensions of organizational environment. The Table 29.2 is showing a grid of organizational environment along with three dimensions that are commitment, relationship and shared values and beliefs.

TABLE 29.2 Dimensions of Organizational Environment

	Shared Values and Beliefs		
Commitment		Low	High
	High	**Ordinary**	**Admirable**
	Low	**Pitiable**	**Ordinary**
		Negative	Positive
	Relationships		

Commitment

In performing cultures all the employees are committed to the DNA of the organization. They are actually allowed to participate in mission development activities because commitment cannot be generated without participation. Commitment also deals with alignment of the employees with a strategic vision of the organization and strong belief on organizational values. Higher commitment enables employees to make effective decisions and follow common approaches. It develops mutual as well as individual accountability towards all the decisions and outcomes. Because of the psychological energy generated through commitment the motivation level of the employees goes up and that makes leaders' job a lot easier. Employee turnover can also be mitigated by enhancing employees' commitment with organizational DNA.

Relationships

Positive relationship means people have affection with each other and they all are bounded by the glue of mutual trust. There exists a creative cooperation among people of the organization and they sacrifice their needs for each other. With creative compromise they form apex and create synergy in the environment. They are ready to take each other's responsibility quite happily and respect everyone's voice in the organization. Leadership roles can be rotated quite easily in the positive relationship environment.

Shared Values and Beliefs

As discussed earlier that people's behaviour is guided by their values and beliefs and as a leader if you can induce organizational values in them, you can develop the desired behaviour in the organization. In the present time, no organization can survive for long without ethical values. Writing ethical values in the policy statements or on the walls of the organization are not going to help much unless it is reflected from the behaviour of the employees. So it is necessary that organizational values and beliefs should be shared widely by all the employees of the organization. Based on these three dimensions, Table 29.2 shows the environment ranging from pitiable, ordinary to admirable.

Ordinary environment

If employees' commitment with organization's mission and objectives is high, but they do not share organization's values with negative relationships among them then the environment is pretty ordinary. Same is the case if values are not shared even if the commitment is high and relationships are positive.

Pitiable environment

The environment becomes pitiable if the organization is not qualifying in all the three dimensions.

Admirable environment

The real congenial environment is admirable environment when employees' commitment with organizational mission and goals are very high; they are aligned with strategic direction; they share organizational values and beliefs in their heart and it is reflected in their behaviour; and they have positive relationships among them. In fact, this is the situation where all the employees are highly committed to the organizational DNA and having a sense of ownership, and sense of achievement and so forth. This situation generates required psychological energy in the environment.

HIGH PERFORMANCE CULTURE ON THE BASIS OF ADMIRABLE ENVIRONMENT AND POSITIVE PERFORMANCE

Having admirable environment is not enough; real high performance organizational cultures ensure higher productivity through positive performance. Table 29.3 shows four types of organizational cultures based on organizational environment and performance.

TABLE 29.3 High Performance Organizational Culture

		Admirable Situation	*Pitiable Situation*
Performance	*Positive*	High performance culture	Dictatorial culture
	Decline	Fruitless culture	Frightening culture

Dictatorial Culture

In this type of culture, there are negative relationships between managers and subordinates, but despite of negative relationships the organizational performance is positive. Goals set by the boss without consultation with employees. There is one way communication that is mainly downward communication. Managers allow their subordinates to participate in decision-making according to their own needs. Managers are involved in managing through their status and position. There are very few learning opportunities for subordinates. In this culture, there exists restrictive job boundaries and training for employees. Employees work with a mindset that the boss knows better. Quality inspectors check on conformance to standards. Quality is the managers' responsibility. People get on with their job with little contact with other departments and customers. People do not challenge the views or ideas of their bosses and fear challenging their managers. Management sets strict rules and checks on people all the time.

Frightening Culture

This type of culture demonstrates negative relationships between managers and subordinates and there exists the declining trends in organizational performance. The boss demands performance without communicating clear goals. They maintain secrecy in the organization and do not trust people with information. Communication among employees and between managers and subordinates is restrictive and due to this reason lot of rumours prevails in the environment.

Subordinates are not allowed to participate in decision-making process. The managers are coercive with people. Workforce is seen as lazy. No trust and little responsibility given to people. People hide poor quality or waste and some times do not care about achieving standards. Departments do not cooperate and blame one another for poor performance. Criticism occurs behind people's back—real fear to speak openly. There is lot of focus on catching people doing things wrong. People hide mistakes.

Fruitless Culture

The warm and ineffective culture is characterized by positive relationship between managers and subordinates, but declining performance trends in the organization. The goals are agreed mutually but no real measures are developing to achieve the same. The employees possess no accountability towards goal achievement. There exists communication among people but it is sporadic and ineffective. Time is wasted in useless talks. In order to make subordinates happy, managers are always talking nicely and telling only good news. The people are more involved in lip-service participation means lots of talks and little action. Poor performances are not confronted there are lots of excuses for poor service and quality. Effectiveness in achieving goals and service levels is not measured. Ineffective departments are not challenged. People are complacent and nice to one another—they avoid conflict. People all appear busy but achieve little. They are more involved in measuring the activities not a result.

High Performance Organizational Culture

In the high performance organizational culture, there exists a positive relationship among the people of the organization. This relationship goes much beyond working relationships reaching into the heart of people and generates mutual commitment for each other. Because of this intense commitment people start caring for each other, become compassionate and are willing to take each other's responsibility. Also they feel themselves accountable for each other's success and failures. All the employees are strongly aligned and involve emotionally with organization's vision, mission, goals, and values. The organizational performance is positive and growing with required pace.

There is effective participation of employees in decision making process, and goals are determined mutually. Employees are asked to decide the organizational focus by developing the organizational mission. Effective measures are mutually developed to achieve the goals. Effective two-way communication prevails in the system. There exists democratic and open climate in the organization, and transparency in all actions is maintained. People are empowered to take decisions and frame their short-term goals. There are self-directed teams that monitor, and continually improve their performance. Everyone can make a contribution and is an expert in his/her own right. Quality and service are the responsibility of the person doing the job. Supply-chain integration and customer focused goals prevail across all functions. Ideas are shared freely. People feel free to disagree without fear of victimization. All are concerned with results and outputs. People are innovative in how they do their work to achieve agreed goals. The high performance organizational culture is adaptive in nature where managers pay close attention to all the stakeholders of the organization and develop partnership with them. Leadership at all levels is valued; people are encouraged to provide leadership and initiate change whenever needed to satisfy the legitimate interests of those stakeholders.

Values within the departments in the high performance organizational culture:

- Mutual trust.
- Mutual respect.
- Colleagues who have the guts to say it.
- Mutual protection against foreign forces.
- Genuine consensus and synergy.
- No false behaviour that seeks to impress.
- Absolute communication and sharing of information.
- If you are annoyed with me, tell me first.
- No departmental isolation and power positioning.
- A collective spirit which protects the values.
- Time for one another, regular discussion, and fun.
- A feeling that "we are here to serve the world".
- Believe in that real satisfaction comes from sacrificing the needs and not from satisfying the needs.
- Believe in nurturing leadership.

The way we do things around in high performance organizational culture

We place customer service first, we trust and respect each other, we are totally committed to quality, we adhere to the highest standards of integrity, we must achieve excellent performance, and we have pride in belonging to our organization.

Organizational Transcendence

As described earlier in Section II, Chapter 16 under the heading spirituality, a person can generate very high excellence in his work if he becomes self-transcendent by getting detached from greed, envy, desires, future gains and losses, and by embracing sense of contribution, integration, and acquiring knowledge to serve the society. The same philosophy applies in high performance organizational culture. The gracious work culture can transform normal performing organizations into transcendent organizations.

Gracious Work Culture

In transcendent organizations all the people are in mode of graciousness. The transcendental qualities that exist in gracious work culture are fearlessness; purification of one's existence; cultivation of spiritual knowledge; charity; self-control; performance of sacrifice; austerity; simplicity; non-violence; truthfulness; freedom from anger and anxiety; calmness; aversion to fault finding; compassion for all living entities; freedom from materialism; gentleness; modesty; steady determination; heartiness; forgiveness; resilience; cleanliness; and freedom from envy and from passion for honour.

People in gracious work culture are liberated and become fearless, pure, and simple. They develop self-control and become free from personal needs and desires. They develop sense of contribution and everything becomes meaningful for them as they want to love and tender their service to society without any expectation.

These transcendental qualities in the organizational culture can generate excellence in the organizational performances and these organizations satisfy their association and escalation needs (as described in Chapter 10) with very high amplitude.

Why Change in Organizational Culture is Difficult?

The culture within an organization usually helps to support the current power structure, and therefore, the power structure usually fights any change that might threaten its privileges and power status. Cultures are perpetuated by a variety of mechanisms within the organization. If the appraisal, rewards, and promotion system in the organization are not revamped in some way, these will slowly undermine any change efforts. Because culture touches human values, changing culture causes strong emotions; fear of losing people will cling harder to familiar and fight to keep the status quo so that they can remain in their comfort zones.

HOW TO BRING CHANGES IN ORGANIZATIONAL CULTURE?

Start working from the DNA of the organization. Diagnose current DNA of your organization. Find the fit between organizational and personal values. Assess the preferred DNA for stakeholders. Envision future culture. Create an atmosphere of perceived "crisis" in the organization. Without dissatisfaction with current state, there is little incentive for managers to change familiar pattern of behaviour. Develop, clarify and communicate the vision widely and repeatedly. Ask your employees to set the purpose of the organizations. Model through your own actions, the kinds of values and practices you want to induce into your firm. Empower the people, look for some quick but sustainable success, celebrate small wins, and demonstrate patience and persistence.

Criteria for Successful Cultural Change

- Existing culture blocks need to be removed.
- Change agents have influence and freedom to act.
- Resources available—time, people, money and equipment.
- Early performance decrease must be tolerated.
- Top management should be actively engaged in the process of cultural change, because culture comes from top.
- Acceptance of managers that changes are needed.
- Willingness to experience culture shock.
- Patience and time.

Key Factor in Culture Change

- Understand the old culture.
- Encourage people to change the old culture and reward those with new ideas.
- Recognize outstanding units in the organization, and use them as model for change.

Do not impose culture change

- Let employees be involved in finding their new approaches to change and an improved culture will emerge.
- Lead with a vision, the vision provides guiding principles for change, but must be bought into by employees.

Large-scale change takes time

- It may take three to five years for organization-wide cultural changes to take significant effect.

Live the new culture

- Top management values, behaviours, and actions will speak louder than words.

The real problem with leaders today is that they are not assertive enough in trying to influence the behaviour of people around them. As a result, they are not influencing the companies as much as they could. Through upholding the culture, leaders should influence assertively how employees should behave. As a leader, you must make sure that desired behaviour of employees should reach to their unconscious competence and becomes a habit because culture is what people do when no one is telling them what to do. Organizational culture is commonly held in the mind framework of organizational members.

APPENDICES

APPENDIX

1

Leadership Qualities

Name of the Participant:

Total Marks Obtained:

1.	When I am involved in serious disagreement, I do not hang in there to waste my time to resolve the issue.	YES	Partially YES	NO
2.	I prefer to call people in my room to solve the problems rather to go to their rooms.	YES	Partially YES	NO
3.	I do not prefer to include many people in the activities or discussions.	YES	Partially YES	NO
4.	While solving the problem I do not allow group's interference because they can distract my attention.	YES	Partially YES	NO
5.	I would prefer to promote conventional beliefs, values and methods over non-conventional ones.	YES	Partially YES	NO
6.	I will prefer compliance over inspiring trust from people in the organization.	YES	Partially YES	NO
7.	I will not verbalize the higher values than that of organization stands for.	YES	Partially YES	NO
8.	I will not prefer new and unique ways of doing things over traditionally identified best ways.	YES	Partially YES	NO
9.	I cannot cheer people up when my own spirits are down.	YES	Partially YES	NO
10.	My personal achievements are equally important than my team's achievements.	YES	Partially YES	NO
11.	To avoid unnecessary nuisance I do not involve myself in my teammates' problems.	YES	Partially YES	NO
12.	I do not see reasons to convince everyone in the organization.	YES	Partially YES	NO

Instructions for Researcher

The proposed questionnaire can be used for assessing the quality of a person as a Leader.

Scoring

YES = 1, Partially YES = 2, NO = 3

Interpretation

Above 90% = Excellent leadership qualities

Between 80–89% = Good leadership qualities

Between 70–79% = Average leadership qualities

Below 69% = Lot of work to be done.

Instructions

1. Select the samples from diverse units randomly.
2. Ensure that each selected unit is participating with equal number of samples.
3. The sample unit must be educated enough to understand the questions.
4. Use scheduling method. This means do not handover this questionnaire to respondents rather you ask each question with your respondents and note down their response. This is because they may not understand the questions fully.
5. Translate the questions into simple Hindi language (if required) while asking the respondents in order to make them easy to understand.

(Questionnaire to assess leadership qualities, developed by Dr. Sanjay Saxena, Reader, Department of Management, and Chief Trainer, Leadership Training Centre, School of Management Sciences, Varanasi, UP India.)

APPENDIX

Emotional Autonomy

Name of the Participant:

Total Marks Obtained:

1.	I know when I am becoming angry.	5	4	3	2	1
2.	I know in what sense I am talking in.	5	4	3	2	1
3.	I can easily identify when I experience mood shift.	5	4	3	2	1
4.	I know when I am defensive.	5	4	3	2	1
5.	I can calm myself quickly when angry.	5	4	3	2	1
6.	I can keep myself relaxed under pressure situation.	5	4	3	2	1
7.	I always talk to myself internally to change my emotional state.	5	4	3	2	1
8.	I can stay calm when others are shouting on me.	5	4	3	2	1
9.	I know when I am thinking negatively.	5	4	3	2	1
10.	"Gear up" at will for a task.	5	4	3	2	1
11.	I can recover quickly after a setback.	5	4	3	2	1
12.	I can change my ineffective or bad habit.	5	4	3	2	1
13.	Produce motivation when doing uninteresting work.	5	4	3	2	1
14.	I follow my words with action.	5	4	3	2	1

Instructions for Researcher

The proposed questionnaire can be used for assessing the leader's emotional autonomy state.

Interpretation

Above 90% = Excellent emotional autonomy

Between 80 – 89% = Good emotional autonomy

Between 70 – 79% = Average emotional autonomy

Below 69% = Lot of work to be done.

(Questionnaire to assess leader's emotional autonomy, developed by Dr. Sanjay Saxena, Reader, Department of Management, and Chief Trainer, Leadership Training Centre, School of Management Sciences, Varanasi, UP India.)

APPENDIX

3

Emotional Reciprocation

Name of the Participant:

Total Marks Obtained:

1.	To avoid any mishap I want to be reserved at workplace.	5	4	3	2	1
2.	I tell others what they want to hear rather emphasizing the truth.	5	4	3	2	1
3.	I have trouble expressing my feelings.	5	4	3	2	1
4.	I became uneasy when others are expressing their feelings about the organization or a particular situation.	5	4	3	2	1
5.	I cannot recognize when others are distressed.	5	4	3	2	1
6.	I do not engage myself in intimate conversation with others.	5	4	3	2	1
7.	I harass and intimidate others too frequently.	5	4	3	2	1
8.	I make negative comments about group members too readily.	5	4	3	2	1
9.	I like to tell about my accomplishments and qualities to others quite often.	5	4	3	2	1
10.	Sometimes I do not mind breaking my commitments for more important work or if it is not going to harm me.	5	4	3	2	1

(*Contd.*)

11.	I try to save my travelling time by congratulating others for their achievements or expressing sorrow for their painful events on phone.	5	4	3	2	1
12.	I would like to ensure recognition for my sincere efforts before the credit is given to the team.	5	4	3	2	1
13.	I do not believe in small courtesies instead I believe in straightforward give and take business.	5	4	3	2	1
14.	I do not want to develop affection with my employees otherwise they can exploit my emotions.	5	4	3	2	1

Instructions for Researcher

The proposed questionnaire can be used for assessing the leader's interpersonal skills.

Scoring

5 = 1, 4 = 2, 3 = 3, 2 = 4, and 1 = 5

Interpretation

Above 90% = Excellent interpersonal skills

Between 80 – 89% = Good interpersonal skills

Between 70 – 79% = Average interpersonal skills

Below 69% = Lot of work to be done.

(Questionnaire to assess leader's interpersonal skills, developed by Dr. Sanjay Saxena, Reader, Department of Management, and Chief Trainer, Leadership Training Centre, School of Management Sciences, Varanasi, UP India.)

APPENDIX

Change Agent

Name of the Participant:

Total Marks Obtained:

1.	I do not encourage people to frequently express ideas and opinions that differ from my own.	A	B	C	D	E
2.	How can I give prize for initiatives, if the final outcome is disappointing?	A	B	C	D	E
3.	I do not take risks or encourage others to take risks if chances of failure are there.	A	B	C	D	E
4.	I spend time developing new ways of approaching old problems.	A	B	C	D	E
5.	I only complement others on changes they have made if the significance level is high.	A	B	C	D	E
6.	I cannot involve myself in multiple improvements in my personality at a time.	A	B	C	D	E
7.	I do not waste my time to listen to people's idea, if those are stupid.	A	B	C	D	E
8.	I can't spend huge amount of money only for ideas.	A	B	C	D	E

(*Contd.*)

9.	I always try to stabilize and reduce uncertainty in my life.	A	B	C	D	E
10.	I always try to reduce future uncertainty before taking any decision.	A	B	C	D	E
11.	I do not make changes if I do not see any reason to change.	A	B	C	D	E
12.	I feel happy when everything is running well and no change is required.	A	B	C	D	E

A = Completely agree

B = Agree

C = Partially agree

D = Disagree

E = Completely disagree

Instructions for Researcher

The proposed questionnaire can be used for assessing the quality of a person as a change agent. Good leaders are actually excellent change agents therefore, the persons sitting on key positions must possess the change agent's qualities.

Scoring

A= 1, B = 2, C = 3, D = 4, E = 5

Interpretation

Above 90% = Excellent change agent

Between 80–89% = Good change agent

Between 70–79% = Average change agent

Below 69% = Lots of work to be done.

(Questionnaire to assess leadership qualities as change agent, developed by Dr. Sanjay Saxena, Reader, Department of Management, and Chief Trainer, Leadership Training Centre, School of Management Sciences, Varanasi, UP India.)

APPENDIX

Assessment of Leadership Practices in the Organization

Name of the Participant:

Total Score:

1.	When managers are involved in serious disagreement, they hang in there to resolve the issue.	A	B	C	D	E
2.	The managers prefer to call people in their room to solve the problems rather to go to them.	A	B	C	D	E
3.	They believe in written papers rather than trusting their employees.	A	B	C	D	E
4.	They build consensus with others.	A	B	C	D	E
5.	They take the decision and tell people to follow the same.	A	B	C	D	E
6.	They give memos if employees are not working satisfactorily.	A	B	C	D	E
7.	They calm themselves quickly when angry.	A	B	C	D	E
8.	They encourage new ideas and new techniques of doing things over traditional ones.	A	B	C	D	E
9.	The initiatives are rewarded even if the outcomes are not satisfactory.	A	B	C	D	E

(*Contd.*)

10.	Do you know the vision of your organization? If yes, then how much you believe in it?	A	B	C	D	E
11.	Do you know the mission of your organization? If yes, then how much you believe in it?	A	B	C	D	E
12.	Do you know the values of your organization? If yes, in then how much you believe them?	A	B	C	D	E
13.	People do not criticize on each other's back.	A	B	C	D	E
14.	You feel yourself responsible for other's job too.	A	B	C	D	E
15.	Everyone in your unit follow the common approach to perform the job.	A	B	C	D	E
16.	People trust each other.	A	B	C	D	E
17.	People cooperate each other to achieve individual targets.	A	B	C	D	E

A = Completely agree
B = Agree
C = Partially agree
D = Disagree
E = Completely disagree

Instructions for Researcher

This questionnaire is designed to assess the leadership practices in any organization. The sample unit should be subordinates in the organization because they can reflect the real picture of leadership practices in the organization.

Scoring

A= 5, B = 4, C = 3, D = 2, E = 1.

Interpretation

Above 90% = Excellent leadership in the environment

Between 80 – 89% = Good leadership in the environment

Between 70 – 79% = Average leadership in the environment

Below 69% = Lot of work to be done.

1. The question number 1 – 9 assesses the leadership qualities of the persons holding key positions in the organization.

2. The question number 10 to 17 assesses the work-environment of the organization reflecting the success of leaders in developing the same.
3. As a researcher you can assess the scoring percentage on each item included in the questionnaire in order to find the development needs in the organization.

Instructions

1. Fix the minimum sample size to 200.
2. Select the samples from diverse units randomly.
3. Ensure that each selected unit is participating with equal number of samples.
4. The sample unit must be educated enough to understand the questions.
5. Use scheduling method. This means do not handover this questionnaire to respondents rather you ask each question with your respondents and note down their response. This is because they may not understand the questions fully.
6. Translate the questions into simple Hindi language while asking with respondents in order to make them easy to understand.

(Questionnaire to assess leadership qualities, developed by Dr. Sanjay Saxena, Reader, Department of Management, and Chief Trainer, Leadership Training Centre, School of Management Sciences, Varanasi, UP India.)

APPENDIX

Assessment of Team Effectiveness

Name of the Participant:

Total Score:

1.	There are regular group meetings.	A	B	C	D	E
2.	Group vision is clearly defined and communicated to all the group members.	A	B	C	D	E
3.	We talked about and shared the same goals for group work and grade.	A	B	C	D	E
4.	Our discussions are active and open-ended.	A	B	C	D	E
5.	We do not stop communication until the conflicts and disagreements are resolved.	A	B	C	D	E
6.	We listen to each other with empathy.	A	B	C	D	E
7.	We trust each other and speak freely.	A	B	C	D	E
8.	Leadership roles are rotated and shared, with people taking initiative at appropriate times for the good of the group.	A	B	C	D	E
9.	Each member finds a way to contribute to the final work product.	A	B	C	D	E
10.	We freely give each other credit for jobs well done.	A	B	C	D	E

(*Contd.*)

11.	Group members give and receive feedback to help the group to do better.	A	B	C	D	E
12.	Each member is accountable to the group.	A	B	C	D	E
13.	Group members are maintaining each other's dignity.	A	B	C	D	E

A = Completely agree,
B = Agree,
C = Partially agree,
D = Disagree,
E = Completely disagree

Instructions for Researcher

This questionnaire is designed to assess the team leadership in any organization. The sample unit should be team members of a particular team in the organization because they can reflect the real picture of leadership practices in their team.

Scoring

A= 5, B = 4, C = 3, D = 2, E = 1.

Scoring and Interpretation for Team Cohesiveness

The questions here are about team cohesiveness.

- If the score is 52 or greater, the group experiences authentic team work.
- If the score is between 39 and 51, there is a positive team identity that might have been developed even further.
- If the score is between 26 and 38, team identity is weak and probably not very satisfying.
- If the score is below 26, it is hardly a team at all, resembling more a loose collection of individuals.

(Questionnaire to assess team effectiveness, developed by Dr. Sanjay Saxena, Reader, Department of Management, and Chief Trainer, Leadership Training Centre, School of Management Sciences, Varanasi, UP India.)

References

Bandura A., *Social Foundation of Thought and Action: A Social Cognitive Theory,* Prentice-Hall, Englewood Cliffs, N.J., 1986.

Bowen E. David and Lawler E. Edward III, "Empowering Service Employees," *Sloan Management Review,* Summer 1995.

Cherie Carter–Scott, *Negaholics: How to Overcome Negativity and Turn Your Life Around,* Random House Publishing Group, New York, 1999.

Covey R. Stephen, *The Seven Habits of Highly Effective People,* Simon & Schuster UK Ltd., London, 1989.

Csikszentimihalyi M., *Flow: The Psychology of Optimal Experience,* Harper and Row, New York, 1990.

Drucker F. Peter, *Managing for the Future: The 1990s and Beyond,* Truman Talley Books/Dutton, New York, 1992.

DuBrin J. Andrew, *Leadership: Research Findings, Practice, and Skills,* Houghton Mifflin Company, Boston, 1995.

Eleanor Roosevelt, *This is My Story*, Harper and Brothers, New York, 1937.

Fiedler E. Fred, "The Efforts of Leadership Training and Experience: A Contingency Model Interpretation," *Administrative Science Quarterly*, 17, 1972.

Frankl E. Victor, *Man's Search for Meaning,* Washington Square Press, New York, 1984.

Hambrick Donald, Nadler David, and Tushman Michael, *Navigating Change* McGraw-Hill, Sydney, 1997.

Hersey Paul and Blanchard H. Kenneth, *Management of Organization Behaviour: Utilizing Human Resources,* 5th ed., Prentice-Hall, Englewood Cliffs, NJ, 1988.

Hershey Robert, "A Practitioner's View of Motivation", *Journal of Managerial Psychology* (Volume: 8, Issue: 3), MCB UP Limited, 1993.

Herzberg Frederick, "One More Time: How Do You Motivate Employees?" *Harvard Business Review*, January–February 1968.

House J. Robert and Mitchell R. Terence, "Path-Goal Theory of Leadership", *Journal of Contemporary Business*, Autumn 1974.

Ibarra Herminia, "Networking is Vital for Successful Managers," *Ambition: The Newsletter of Association of MBAs*, Issue-8, October–December, London, 2008.

Katzenbach R. John and Smith K. Douglas, "The Discipline of Teams," *Harvard Business Review*, March–April 1993.

Katzenbach R. John and Smith K. Douglas, "The Wisdom of Teams", *Collins Business Essentials Edition*, 2006.

Kenneth A. Kovach, *Organization Size, Job Satisfaction, Absenteeism, and Turnover,* University Press of America, N.H., 1978.

Khera S., *You Can Win,* Macmillan India, Delhi, 2002.

Kotter P. John, "What Leaders Really Do," *Harvard Business Review*, May–June 1990.

Kotter P. John, *A Force of Change: How Leadership Differs from Management,* Free Press, New York, 1990.

Kotter P. John, *Leading Change: Why Transformations Fail?"* Harvard Business School Press, Boston, 1996.

Maslow F. Abraham, A Theory of Human Motivation, *Psychological Review-50,* 1943.

McClelland C. David, *The Two Faces of Power in Organizational Psychology* Prentice-Hall, Englewood Cliffs, N.J., 1971.

Mehrabian A., *Silent Messages,* Wadsworth, Belmont, California, 1971.

Missirian A.K. (Ed.), reprinted in *The Case of Corporate Woman,* Prentice-Hall, New York, 1981.

Morgan P.B. Scott, "Barriers to a High Performance Business", *Management Review*, July 1993.

Nasser E. Martin and Vivier F. J., *Mindset for the New Generation Organization,* Juta & Company, South Africa, 1995.

Okawa Ryuho, *Invincible Thinking: There is no such thing as defeat,* Jaico Publishing House, Mumbai, 2007.

Peter Koestenbaun, *Leadership: The Inner Side of Greatness,* Jossey-Bass, San Francisco, 1991.

Prabhupada S., *Bhagavad Gita As It Is,* Shaktivedanta Book Trust, Mumbai, 2003.

Ralph M. Stogdill, *Handbook of Leadership: A Survey of Theory and Research,* Free Press, New York, 1971.

Robert E. Kelly, *The Power of Followership,* Doubleday, New York, 1992.

Robinson W. James, Jack Welch, *Jack Welch and Leadership: Executive Lessons from the Master CEO,* Forum Publishing, South Florida, 2001.

Rost C. Joseph, *Leadership for the Twenty-First Century,* Praeger, Westport, CN, 1993.

Rothschild William, *Risktaker, Caretaker, Surgeon, Undertaker: The Four Faces of Strategic Leadership,* John Wiley, New York, 1993.

Rotter, J.B. "Generalized Expectations of internal versus external control of reinforcements," *Psychological Monographs-80*, Princeton, 1966.

Ryuzaburo Kaku, "The Path of Kyosei", *Harvard Business Review*, Vol. 75, July-August 1997.

Schein H. Edgar, "Organizational Culture," *American Psychologist 45*, No. 2, February 1990.

Schermerhorn R. John Jr., Osborn N. Richard, and Hunt G. James, *Core Concepts of Organizational Behaviour,* John Wiley and Sons, N.J., 2003.

Spreitzer M. Gretchen, "Psychological Empowerment in the Workplace: Dimensions, Measurement, Validation," *Academy of Management Journal* 38 (5), San Francisco, 1995.

Stogdill M. Ralph and Coons E. Advin (Eds.), *Leader Behaviour: Its Description and Measurement,* Bureau of Business Research, The Ohio State University, Columbus, Ohio, 1957.

The Golden Sayings of Epictetus, edited by John Mark, Ockerbloom (onlinebooks@pobox.upenn.edu).

Tony Blair, British Prime Minister's Press Conference, October 2000.

Vroom H. Victor and Jago G. Arthur, *The New Leadership: Managing Participation in Organizations,* Prentice-Hall, Englewood Cliffs NJ, 1988.

Warren Bennis and Nanus Burt, "The Leadership Tightrope," *Success*, March 1985.

William James, *The Will to Believe,* Courier Dover Publications, New York, 1956.

Web References

http://rescomp.stanford.edu/cheshire/Einstein_quotes.html

http://www.brainyquote.com/authers/m/mother_teresa.html

http://www.brainyquote.com/quotes/authers/m/mohandas_gandhi.html

http://www.viewonbudhhism.org/resources/buddhist_quotes.html

http://www.woopidoo.com/business_quotes/authors/mahatma-gandhi/index.htm

Index

Accountability, 155
Acumen
    emotional, 70–71
    mental, 64
    physical, 58, 62
Affection, 98
Aligning, 15
Alignment, 34, 117
Articulation, 61
Artifacts, 58
Assertion, 101–102
Attitude, 75
Autonomy, 145

Behaviour
    aggressive, 88
    assertive, 87–88
    passive, 87
Behavioural engineering, 56
Body language, 60
Broad-based action, 164
Bureaucracy, 150

Change, 158, 161, 177
Change agent, 11, 189
Change process, 163
Change resistant organizations, 159
Change sensitive organizations, 159
Change vision, 164
Charisma, 28
Coaching, 129–130
Cohesive environment, 105
Collective dependence, 36
Commitment for excellence, 138
Common approach, 136, 140
Communication, 59
Compassionate, 97
Competence ladder, 109
Complacency, 158
Conscious competence, 109
Conscious incompetence, 109
Considerations, 31
Contribution, 91
Cooperation, 99
Core values, 73, 80
    commitment, 81, 98, 123
    concern for others, 80
    harmony, 80
    honesty, 81
    individual dignity, 81
Courtesy, 100
Creative compromise, 100
Creative cooperation, 99
Creative human resource management, 44

Credibility, 96, 163
Criticism, 76
Culture
  dictatorial, 174
  frightening, 174
  fruitless, 175
Culture for excellence, 169

Decision retrieval, 156
Demographic evolution, 160
Demotivators, 148
Denial, 122
Detachment, 90
Discipline, 77
Dysfluency, 61

Emotional autonomy, 71, 185
Emotional condensation, 97
Emotional independency, 71
Emotional reciprocation, 71, 94, 104, 187
  model, 95
Emotional reservoir, 97
Emotional support, 35
Emotional transition, 116, 121
Empathic communication, 162
Empathic listening, 104
Empathy, 101–102
Employee orientation, 19
Empowerment, 153, 155
  boundaries, 156
Environment
  admirable, 173
  ordinary, 173
  pitiable, 173
Envisioning, 28, 33, 117
Excellence in work, 89
Exploration, 123
External adaptation, 169
External focus, 87
Extra mile, 77

Flow, 144
Followers, 22
  conformist, 24
  estranged, 23
  inactive, 24
  situational manipulators, 24
  valuable, 24
Followership patterns, 23

Goals, 74, 135
Gracious work culture, 177
Guiding coalition, 163
Gut instinct, 68

Habits, 108, 110
Harmonizing, 35
High performance culture, 171
High performance organizational culture, 175
High performance organizations, 43
High performance teams, 142
High-performance gracious culture, 44
Humour, 105

Initiating structure, 31
Inspiration, 35
Inspiring, 15
Integrated human being, 21, 56
Integrated production technology, 43
Integration, 92
Internal focus, 87
Internal integration, 169
Internal locus of control, 37
Interpersonal relationship, 97
Interpersonal skills, 104
Intuition, 68
Intuitive skills, 69
Invention, 78
Invincible thinking, 78
Invisible psychological objects, 168
Irrational conclusion, 83

Job enrichment, 147

Leader
  charismatic, 29
  compassionate, 11
  language, 111, 112
  proactive, 10
  transformational, 4, 27, 29
  transactional, 27
Leadership
  autocratic, 19

competences, 108
free-rein style, 19
functions, 115, 116
qualities, 183
situational, 20
strategic, 46
transactional, 27
transformational, 4
Learning opportunities, 146
Learning organizations, 43
Low performance culture, 170

Management by objective, 147
Material nature, 92
Mediator, 105
Meditation, 65
Mentor, 11, 127–128
Mentoring, 35, 127
Mentorship, 127
Micromanagement, 156
Mindset
egocentric, 102
flaccid, 102
stubborn, 102
synergistic, 102–103
Mission, 71, 124, 135
effective, 125
spiritual, 125–126
Mobilization, 34
Mode of graciousness, 94
Mode of lunacy, 93
Mode of obsession, 93
Modesty, 101
Motivation, 143, 145, 150
negative, 18
Motivational construct, 153
Mutual accountability, 136
Mutual cooperation, 140
Mutual feedback, 141
Mutual trust, 95

Needs
association, 42
escalation, 42
organizational, 41–42
subsistence, 42
Nishkaam karma, 91
Non-leader, 10
filtered listening, 11
icy, 11
language, 112
Non-verbal communication, 62

Open climate, 45
Operational networking, 106
Organizational change, 160
Organizational culture, 167–168, 177
Organizational DNA, 16, 124
Organizational environments, 172
Organizational needs, 41
Organizational transcendence, 176
Organizational values, 17

Paralanguage, 60
People orientation, 32
Performance evaluation, 149
Performance results, 136
Persistence, 77
Personal appearance, 59
Personal goals, 75
Personal growth, 135
Personal mission, 71–72
statement, 73–74
Personal paradigm, 55, 57
Persuasion, 151
Physical characteristics, 59
Pitch, 61
Position power, 26
Positive attitude, 75
Positive self-statements, 111
Positive work environment, 146
Power of leaders, 51
Power of vision, 119
Power-distance, 36
Proactive, 112
Proactive language, 86
Proactive model, 86
Proactivity, 85
Psychological empowerment, 153
Psychological energies, 79–80
Psychological entities, 79

Reactive model, 86

Recognition, 157
Relationships, 106–107
Resistance, 122
Resistance to change, 162
Rewards, 157
Roles, 74

Self-awareness, 68
Self-care, 84
Self directing teams, 43
Self-efficacy, 145
Self-esteem, 81, 83
  high, 82
  low, 82
Self-evaluation, 145
Self-monitoring, 144
Self-nurture, 84
Self-perception, 145
Self-systems, 144
Self-transcendence, 94
Sense of achievement, 149
Sense of urgency, 163
Share of heart, 40
Share of wallet, 40
Short-term wins, 165
Sincerity, 99
Skills
  complementary, 134
  decision-making, 135
  interpersonal, 135
  problem solving, 135
  technical, 134
Slack time, 66
Small wins, 141
Spiritual dimensions, 89, 130
Spirituality, 88
Stimulus response theory, 85
Strategic alignment of the firm, 40
Strategic direction, 17, 120
Strategic networking, 107
Strength, 52
Synergistic agreement, 101

Task orientation, 19, 32
Task structure, 25
Teaching, 128–129
Team effectiveness, 194
Team fundamentals, 133
Team norms, 139
Teams, 131
Teamwork, 131, 137–139
Tone, 61
Total quality management, 44
Trustworthy, 96
Two-layer leadership style, 38

Unconscious incompetence, 108
Unconscious mind, 110
Unrealistic generalization, 83

Vague instructions, 149
Value, 79, 176
Visible artifacts, 168
Vision, 118
Voice inflection, 61

Wisdom, 52
World-class organizations, 39
  high performing, 42